WO
on
WOMEN

A. Dillon-Malone is a freelance journalist who contributes to a number of newspapers and magazines, including *Modern Woman*, Ireland's only newspaper for women.

WOMEN

on

WOMEN

and *on* **AGE, BEAUTY, LOVE, MEN, MARRIAGE...**

A. Dillon-Malone

MACMILLAN

First published 1995 by Macmillan Reference Books
a division of Macmillan Publishers Limited
25 Eccleston Place, London SW1W 9NF
and Basingstoke

Associated companies throughout the world

ISBN 0–333–64265–1

9 8 7 6 5 4 3 2 1

A CIP catalogue record for this book is available from the British Library

Phototypeset by Intype, London
Printed and bound in Great Britain
by Cox & Wyman Ltd, Reading, Berkshire

The next best thing to being clever is being able to quote someone who is.

MARY PETTIBONE POOLE

Sometimes it seems the only accomplishment my education ever bestowed on me was the ability to think in quotations.

MARGARET DRABBLE

I might repeat to myself, slowly and soothingly, a list of quotations beautiful from minds profound ... if I can remember any of the damn things.

DOROTHY PARKER

ACKNOWLEDGEMENTS

Special thanks to Mary Dillon-Malone for her continuous encouragement and help; to Margot Davis, Editor of *Modern Woman*, for her perennial enthusiasm; to Judith Hannam of Macmillan for her judicious and unfussy editing; to Chelsey Fox for steering me in the right direction with such buoyancy; and last, but by no means least, to Madeleine for typing the manuscript with such patience after my million and one alterations.

CONTENTS

CONTENTS

INTRODUCTION

THERE WAS once a theatregoer who left a production of *Hamlet* with these words: 'I liked it – but there were too many quotations.' To some, quotes represent trite – and often clichéd – substitutes for life's rich vagaries; for others, they crystallize thoughts and feelings like pearls in oysters.

It is the ambition of this volume to entertain and (hopefully) enlighten. It covers a diverse range of subject matter and biographical revelations, offering opinions on everything from age, beauty and size, to the shortcomings and (occasional) advantages of men. The speakers are all, I might add, female (with the exception of Anon., although many believe he was female too).

In Victorian times, women were seen and not heard. As Jane Austen once put it, 'A woman, especially if she has the misfortune of knowing anything, should conceal it as well as she can.' Pick up any anthology of quotations and a staggering majority of the entries will come from men. This is due to the fact that most anthologists are

(1) sexist in the extreme, (2) lazy, or (3) they simply believe the male of the species is more interesting when it comes to quotable quotes. Certainly this volume shows that (3) is a rather myopic, and unjustified, view.

'One has to secrete a jelly in which to slip a quotation down people's throats,' said Virginia Woolf once, 'and one always secretes too much jelly.' I have tried in the following pages to go easy on the jelly. I would suggest it's a book to be taken up – and dropped – at will. It has a tenuous thematic unity, as indicated by the chapter headings, but such themes dovetail and overlap more often than they don't. The book doesn't attempt to answer any of the conundrums it raises, or to resolve age-old tensions between the sexes. If anything, it asks more questions than it answers.

'Quoting, like smoking, is a dirty habit to which I'm addicted,' says Kate Fansler in *Sweet Death, Kind Death*. Having sifted magpie-like through the flotsam and jetsam of these outpourings, I think I know how she feels.

NOTHING SUCCEEDS LIKE EXCESS

MAN IS the only animal that blushes – or needs to. Just in case you were in any doubt about the fact that human nature is delightfully altruistic, the following chapter should set you straight. Riotous living, bitchy put-downs, sybaritic excess – yes, all the qualities that make life truly noble are contained here.

'When I'm good I'm very good,' said the inimitable Mae West, who could almost have accounted for the whole chapter on her own, 'and when I'm bad I'm even better.' To which Tallulah Bankhead added: 'The only thing I regret about my past is the length of it. If I had to live it over again I'd make the same mistakes, only sooner.'

Bankhead and West are the standard-bearers for the following snippets of debauched indulgence. Perhaps their only redeeming virtue is their honesty – and of course that deliciously irresistible chutzpah.

My life is an open book – all too often at the wrong page.
MAE WEST

I plan to be an appalling old woman. I'm going to boss everyone around. I'll make people stand up for me when I come into a room – and generally capitalize on all the hypocrisy that society shows towards the old.
GLENDA JACKSON

I've always been an alcoholic and I always will be an alcoholic – even if I never touch another drop of booze in my life.
MELANIE GRIFFITH

If you can't invent a really convincing lie, it's often better to stick to the truth.
ANGELA THIRKWELL

The phone went in the house and I answered it and this voice said, 'Hello, how would you like a dirty weekend in Paris?' And then there was a silence and the voice said, 'I'm sorry. Have I shocked you?' And I said, 'God no – I was just packing.'
HELEN LEDERER

I just hate health in general, really. What I hate the most is those natural food shops. What is organic? Just another word for dirty fruit, for God's sake.
RUBY WAX

NOTHING SUCCEEDS LIKE EXCESS

Cocaine isn't habit-forming. I should know — I've been using it for years.

TALLULAH BANKHEAD

Any girl who was a lady would not even think of having such a good time that she did not remember to hang on to her jewellery.

ANITA LOOS

Too much virtue has a corrupting effect.

SUE GRAFTON

Infatuation means a love that is inconvenient to go on with.

CELIA FREMLIN

Don't put the blame where it belongs. Put it where it's easiest to disregard.

JOY FIELDING

I lost my reputation young, but never missed it.

MAE WEST

Even though a number of people have tried, no one has yet found a way to drink for a living.

JEAN KERR

I'm only interested in two kinds of people: those who can entertain me and those who can advance my career.

INGRID BERGMAN

WOMEN ON WOMEN

Until you've lost your reputation, you never really realize what a burden it is.

MARGARET MITCHELL

What stops you killing yourself when you're intoxicated out of your mind is the thought that once you're dead you won't be able to drink any more.

MARGUERITE DURAS

Virtue may be its own reward, but it has no sale at the box office.

MAE WEST

The worst thing about alcoholism is that it's the one disease that tells you you don't have a problem.

HONOR HEFFERNAN

Men aren't attracted to me by my mind, they're attracted by what I *don't* mind.

GYPSY ROSE LEE

You gotta get up early in the morning to catch a fox, and stay up late at night to get a mink.

MAE WEST

I had my first whisky sour at fourteen and thought: God, I've found a friend. But three years ago I thought our friendship was getting too steady, so I gave up.

ELAINE STRITCH

They've called me a scarlet woman for so long I'm almost purple.'

ELIZABETH TAYLOR

The follies which a man regrets most in his life are those which he didn't commit when he had the opportunity.

HELEN ROWLAND

To err is human, but it feels divine.

MAE WEST

I said to this priest, 'Am I expected to believe that if I went out and had an affair, that God was really going to be upset? OK, thou shalt not kill or steal – but thou shalt not commit adultery? If no one is any the wiser, what the hell difference does it make?' But he was lovely. He told me the Commandments were laid down for a lot of guys living in the desert.

DIANA DORS

The idea of strictly minding your own business is mouldy rubbish. Who could be so selfish?

MYRTLE BARKER

I've been on more laps than a napkin.

MAE WEST

There are only three things worthwhile in life – fighting, drinking and making love.

KATHERINE GEROULD

WOMEN ON WOMEN

The best way to get the better of temptation is just to yield to it.

CLEMENTINA GRAHAM

Why should I be good when I'm packing 'em in when I'm bad?

MAE WEST

There's no pleasure in having nothing to do. The pleasure is in having lots to do and not doing it.

MARY WILSON LITTLE

The only original thing about some men is original sin.

HELEN ROWLAND

Playful female mouse seeks shameless male louse.

CLASSIFIED AD

I've been on a calendar, but never on time.

MARILYN MONROE

I have my moments — and they're all weak ones.

MAE WEST

Perhaps the straight and narrow path would be wider if more people used it.

KAY INGRAM

Love your enemy — it will drive him nuts.

ELEANOR DOAN

NOTHING SUCCEEDS LIKE EXCESS

I was brought up in a clergyman's household so I'm a first-class liar.

DAME SYBIL THORNDIKE

Smoking, as far as I'm concerned, is the entire point of being an adult.

FRAN LEBOWITZ

I never hated a man enough to give him his diamonds back.

ZSA ZSA GABOR

My computer-dating bureau came up with a perfect gentleman. Still, I've got another three goes.

SALLY POPLIN

When Woodrow Wilson proposed to me, I was so surprised I nearly fell out of bed.

EDITH BOLTING, on her famous husband

I'm not into working out. My philosophy is: no pain, no pain.

CAROL LIEFER

It's hard to be funny when you have to be clean.

MAE WEST

Nobody speaks the truth when there's something they must have.

ELIZABETH BOWEN

WOMEN ON WOMEN

I lost my virginity as a career move.

MADONNA

The older one grows, the more one likes indecency.

VIRGINIA WOOLF

FOR EVER AND EVER, AH MEN

OK, so Adam was a rough draft, but it wasn't much of a party for Eve either, was it? I'm sure the contemporary woman would have told Adam what to do with his rib. George Bernard Shaw believed that 'this man–woman thing was a stroke of genius on God's part', but the outpourings of the following pages – focusing, as they do, on the inbuilt obsolescence of things amorous – would seem to suggest otherwise. Women sound off on the sexual (and sexist) sins perpetrated by their male counterparts, and the reasons why they can't get on with them (or without them – aye, there's the rub) for any decent period of time. We continue to mate, relate and separate, redefining the delineations of what we want, or need, each time, and still falling on our collective faces after each botched rendezvous as Cupid's little arrows miss their target by the proverbial mile.

It's called chemistry, I think.

WOMEN ON WOMEN

The legend of the jungle heritage and the evolution of the male as a hunting carnivore has taken root in man's mind to such an extent that he believes equal pay will do something terrible to his gonads.

ELAINE MORGAN

More women than ever before in our history are relying on themselves instead of Prince Charming. Work is the vehicle that permits this.

ELIZABETH NICKLES

The great lie of the misnamed sexual revolution has been perhaps to make it [sex] simultaneously more and less important than it is: by divorcing it from the psychic sphere, pretending it is a matter of prowess – and something that can be learned, like tennis.

ROSITA SWEETMAN

There are very few jobs that actually require a penis or vagina. All others should be open to everybody.

FLORYNCE KENNEDY

Ginger Rogers did everything that Fred Astaire did. She just did it backwards and in high heels.

LINDA ELLERBEE

It is not the inferiority of women that has caused their historical insignificance; it is rather their historical insignificance that has doomed them to inferiority.

SIMONE DE BEAUVOIR

FOR EVER AND EVER, AH MEN

The only difference between seduction and rape is that in seduction the rapist bothers to buy a bottle of wine.

ANDREA DWORKIN

The man is a domestic animal which, if treated with firmness and kindness, can be trained to do most things.

JILLY COOPER

Anyone can have the key to the executive washroom, but once a woman gets inside, what is there? A lavatory.

GERMAINE GREER

I'm not denying women are foolish: God made them to match the men.

GEORGE ELIOT

If I had been born a man, I would have conquered Europe. As I was born a woman, I expended my energy on tirades against fate, and eccentricities.

MARIE BASHKIRTSEFF

The only time a woman really succeeds in changing a man is when he's a baby in nappies.

NATALIE WOOD

I'd like to get to the point where I can be just as mediocre as a man.

JUANITA KREPS

I like men to behave like men — strong and childish.

FRANÇOISE SAGAN

WOMEN ON WOMEN

The main difference between a dog and a man is that if you pick up a starving dog and make him prosper he will not bite you.

BARBRA STREISAND

The practice of putting women on pedestals began to die out when it was discovered that they could give orders better from that position.

BETTY GRABLE

If a man does something silly, people say, 'Isn't he silly?' If a woman does something silly, people say, 'Aren't women silly?'

DORIS DAY

The first time Adam had a chance, he laid the blame on a woman.

NANCY ASTOR

The standards women set themselves these days are incredibly high, and we can't live up to them. Whatever we do, we can never make the perfect soufflé and be up in the bedroom in the black lacy underwear. Or if we are, the plumber's bound to be in there.

MAUREEN LIPMAN

Men like to see women as objects: that image of totally contrived sexuality – bleached hair, pushed-up tits and make-up an inch thick – still works.

THERESA RUSSELL

FOR EVER AND EVER, AH MEN

More and more it appears that, biologically, men are destined for short brutal lives – and women for long, miserable ones.

ESTELLE RAMEY

The honeymoon is over when he wants the kitchen in good shape rather than a good shape in the kitchen.

ANON.

Ah, the relationships we get into just to get out of the ones we are not brave enough to say are over.

JULIA PHILLIPS

If a woman has her Ph.D. in Physics, has mastered in quantum theory, plays flawless Chopin, was once a cheerleader, and is now married to a man who plays baseball, she will for ever be 'former cheerleader married to star athlete'.

MARYANNE SIMMONS

By the time he tells you you were made for one another . . . he's already planning alterations.

ANON.

A smart girl is one who knows how to play tennis, golf, piano . . . and dumb.

MARILYN MONROE

Women, children and lunatics can't be Pope.

CARYL CHURCHILL

WOMEN ON WOMEN

Being a woman is of special interest only to aspiring male transsexuals. To actual women, it is merely a good excuse not to play football.

FRAN LEBOWITZ

The problems between myself and Frank Sinatra never started in bed. We were always great in the bedroom. The problems started on the way to the bidet.

AVA GARDNER

Men are like naughty little boys. They want the bar of chocolate they can't have. When they've got it at home, they go out and look for another piece.

JACKIE COLLINS

Some men treat all women as sequels.

ANON.

A woman needs a man like a fish needs a bicycle.

GLORIA STEINEM

Whatever women do, they must do twice as well as men to be thought half as good. Luckily, this isn't difficult.

CHARLOTTE WHITTEN

One is not born a woman, one becomes one.

SIMONE DE BEAUVOIR

Oh God, who does not exist, you hate women. Otherwise you'd have made them different.

EDNA O'BRIEN

FOR EVER AND EVER, AH MEN

I asked my husband to restore my confidence. I told him my boobs were gone, my stomach was gone. I asked him to say something nice about my legs. 'Blue goes with everything,' he said.

JOAN RIVERS

I think being a woman is like being Irish: everyone says you're important and nice, but you take second place all the same.

IRIS MURDOCH

No nice men are good at getting taxis.

KATHERINE WHITEHORN

There are men I could spend eternity with. But not this life.

KATHLEEN NORRIS

The history of men's opposition to women's emancipation is perhaps more interesting than the story of that emancipation itself.

VIRGINIA WOOLF

Any woman who has a great deal to offer the world is in big trouble.

HAZEL SCOTT

There's a vast difference between the savage and civilized man, but it's never apparent to their wives until after breakfast.

HELEN ROWLAND

What is most beautiful in virile men is something feminine; what is most beautiful in feminine women is something masculine.

SUSAN SONTAG

I can trust my husband not to fall asleep on a public platform – and he usually claps in the right places.

MARGARET THATCHER

The more I see of men, the more I admire dogs.

BRIGITTE BARDOT

It wasn't a woman who betrayed Jesus with a kiss.

CATHERINE CARSWELL

To be happy with a man you must understand him a lot and love him a little. To be happy with a woman you must love her a lot and not try to understand her at all.

HELEN ROWLAND

The more I think of men, the less I think of them.

ANON.

Perhaps women have always been in closer contact with reality than men; it would seem to be the just recompense for being deprived of idealism.

GERMAINE GREER

Men are six feet, women are five feet twelve.

MARGAUX HEMINGWAY

FOR EVER AND EVER, AH MEN

Why are women so much more interesting to men than men are to women?

VIRGINIA WOOLF

A woman should never believe a man who says 'I love you' before sex . . . and a man should never believe a woman who says 'I love you' after it.

WENDY DENNIS

All the world's top chefs are men, so the question I want to ask is: 'How come most men claim they can't cook?'

DIANA DORS

Once a woman is made man's equal, she becomes his superior.

MARGARET THATCHER

Men are brought up to command, women to seduce. To admit the necessity of seduction is to admit that one has not the strength to command.

SALLY KEMPTON

Most women need a room of their own — and often the only place to find it is outside their own homes.

GERMAINE GREER

People call me a feminist when I express sentiments that differentiate me from a doormat or a prostitute.

REBECCA WEST

There is nothing as unattractive as a man collapsing at one's feet. Someone who doesn't need us is a lot less scary than someone who needs us too much. So we'll go for a guy who gives us that crucial distance, who forgets to call, fails to buy flowers . . . and has difficulty remembering our name.

CYNTHIA HEIMEL

Women speak because they wish to speak, whereas a man speaks only when driven to speech by something outside himself – like, for instance, he can't find any clean socks.

JEAN KERR

The Paula Principle ensures that women stay below their level of competence and thus are held back from promotion.

LIZ FILKIN

When women are supposed to be quiet, a talkative woman is one who talks at all.

DALE SPENDER

Failing to be there when a man wants her is woman's greatest sin – apart from being there when he doesn't want her.

HELEN ROWLAND

You could put everything I know about men on the head of a pin – and still have room for the Lord's Prayer.

CHER

FOR EVER AND EVER, AH MEN

Yeats ruined my life as a teenage girl. Here was this magnificent beautiful woman, Maud Gonne McBride, depicted as a trollop for having the nerve and awfulness to reject this man. That vision conspired to make me and other women feel that we too were trollops if we wanted to end a relationship and the boy did not.

EVELYN CONLON

A male gynaecologist is like an auto mechanic who never owned a car.

CARRIE SNOW

If the right man does not come along, there are many fates far worse. One is to have the *wrong* man come along.

LETITIA BALDRIGE

Freud is the father of psychoanalysis. It has no mother.

GERMAINE GREER

Women have served all these centuries as looking-glasses, possessing the magic and delicious power of reflecting the figure of man at twice its normal size.

VIRGINIA WOOLF

I don't wish women to have power over men – but over themselves.

SIMONE DE BEAUVOIR

It is hard to fight an enemy who has outposts in your head.

SALLY KEMPTON

WOMEN ON WOMEN

Women fail to understand how much men hate them.

GERMAINE GREER

Where young boys plan for *what* they will achieve and attain, young girls plan for *whom* they will achieve and attain.

CHARLOTTE GILMAN

Mr Gladstone speaks to me as if I were a public meeting.

QUEEN VICTORIA

The most unsatisfactory men are those who pride themselves on their virility, and regard sex as if it were some form of athletics in which you win cups.

MARILYN MONROE

I resent the fact that Prince can get away with thrusting his hips and be called sexy. When I do it, I'm called a bimbo.

WENDY JAMES

Women like the simple things of life – like men.

ANON.

Men generally fall into three categories: the handsome, the clever – and the majority.

MARILYN FRENCH

There's this image of Mother Ireland sending out her sons to fight for her. It's always *Mother* Ireland. You can't be just a woman. You're always either a mother or a sister or a daughter or a wife. You're generally an extension of something else — and it's usually a bloody man.

MAIREAD FARRELL

Nature is not a feminist. If it were, women would have no biological clock and no menopause. Instead of being born with all the eggs we'll ever have, women would produce new eggs until we were eighty. Giving birth would be a breeze, and there would be no such thing as a stretch mark. Men would run out of sperm when they were fifty, whereupon everyone would approve as we dumped our worn-out flabby husbands and scooped up young dudes and started a whole new life.

CYNTHIA HEIMEL

When God made men, she was only joking.

ANON.

In a two-car family, the wife always has the smaller car.

RUTH RENDELL

The best way to solve the problems between the sexes would be to make marriage very difficult and divorce very easy, instead of the reverse.

GLENDA JACKSON

Macho guys don't really go for me. They're frightened of their femininity.

MADONNA

Women will be the weaker sex as long as they're strong enough to get away with it.

ANON.

You see an awful lot of smart guys with dumb women, but you hardly ever see a smart woman with a dumb guy.

ERICA JONG

Modern drugs are wonderful. They enable a wife with pneumonia to nurse her husband through flu.

JILLY COOPER

Women have a lot of faults, but men only two: everything they say and everything they do.

LEONORA STRUMPFENBURG

The average guy has a pathetic body, and when guys like that see me they feel threatened.

MARTINA NAVRATILOVA

I didn't leave Sonny for another man. I left him for another woman. Me.

CHER

Women spend a lot of time and energy minding men's egos. It's like living with a corn on your foot all the time.

RHONA TEEHAN

The male is an incomplete female, a walking abortion, aborted at the gene stage. To be male is to be deficient, emotionally crippled. Maleness is a deficiency disease and males are emotionally crippled.

VALERIE SOLANAS

Adolf doesn't even take his boots off, and sometimes we don't get into the bed. We stretch out on the floor. On the floor he is very erotic.

EVA BRAUN, on Hitler

Clark Gable always remembered my birthday, and my fiftieth was coming up and he said, 'I want to give you a party.' And I said, 'Well that's very darling of you.' He said, 'All right, let's say eight o'clock on the evening of your birthday.' So he sent a car for me and I got to his home and there wasn't a soul anywhere in sight and I said, 'Where's the party?' and he said, 'Well look, you don't think I'm going to waste your fiftieth birthday with a lot of strange people running round here? You can always say for the rest of your life, to your grandchildren and everybody, you can always say you spent your fiftieth birthday in bed with Clark Gable!'

ADELA ROGERS ST JOHN

It used to be boy meets girl, boy falls in love with girl, boy marries girl. Now it's boy meets girl, boy goes to bed with girl, boy and girl analyse one another's feelings, boy decides he's not ready for a commitment and girl says she needs her 'space' . . . and boy and girl split. But not before one last bonk.

SHARON DWYER

WOMEN ON WOMEN

We were discussing the possibility of making one of our cats Pope recently and we decided that the fact that she was not Italian and was female made the third point — that she was a cat — quite irrelevant.

VIRGINIA WOOLF

You can run an office without a boss, but not without secretaries.

JANE FONDA

Blessed is the man who, having nothing to say, abstains from giving wordy evidence of that fact.

GEORGE ELIOT

A woman has got to love a bad man once or twice in her life to be thankful for a good one.

MARJORIE RAWLINGS

If you never want to see a man again, say 'I love you. I want to marry you. I want to have children'. They leave skid marks.

RITA RUDNER

I hate humanity. I'm allergic to it. Men are beasts, and even beasts don't behave that badly. If I could do anything about the way people behave I would, but since I can't I'll stick to animals.

BRIGITTE BARDOT

FOR EVER AND EVER, AH MEN

You just leave those Russians to me, honey. I'll take 'em all on, a battalion at a time, and send them back to Omsk with their little tails between their legs.

MAE WEST

Scratch a New Man and you'll find a hypocritical old one. The New Man merely uses his fake sensitivity as a sophisticated form of foreplay.

MARY MANNION

A woman wrote to me once telling me she had gone to her boyfriend's home to wait for him after he had told her he had to work late. She found no lights on. After she entered the darkened house with her key, her boyfriend emerged from the bedroom and pretended he had fallen asleep. When she went into his bedroom, she found a woman hiding in his closet. He vigorously denied that anything had occurred and claimed the woman had gone into the closet because she was scared.

CAROL BOTWIN

I don't think I could ever fancy a man who had to disappear to the men's room to touch up his lipstick.

DIANA DORS

To be able to turn a man out into a garden and tell him to stay there until the next meal is every woman's dream.

VIRGINIA GRAHAM

The hardest task in a girl's life is to prove to a man that his intentions are serious.

HELEN ROWLAND

A woman can walk through the Louvre Museum in Paris and see 5,000 breathtaking paintings on the wall. A man can walk through the Louvre Museum and see 5,000 nails in the wall. That's the difference between the sexes.

ERMA BOMBECK

Boy, am I exhausted. I went on a double date last night and the other girl didn't show up.

MAE WEST

Once a woman has forgiven her man, she must not reheat his sins for breakfast.

MARLENE DIETRICH

Men always fall for frigid women because they put on the best show.

FANNY BRICE

In Vienna, a woman found pictures of another woman in her husband's wallet. Recognizing the nude girl as her supposed best friend, she had each of the photographs blown up to poster size and pasted them up around the city with captions like 'Behold the adulteress' and 'Lock up your husband when you see this woman'. She ended up in court on a charge of displaying obscene photographs and was given a token five days' imprisonment. When she came out she was reconciled with her husband.

SHIRLEY ESKAPA

The best place to find single men these days is the frozen food section of the supermarket, around 7 p.m.

OPRAH WINFREY

I view with deep suspicion any man who actually looks forward to going to the hairdresser.

BERYL DOWNING

I became a feminist as an alternative to becoming a masochist.

SALLY KEMPTON

If I found him with another woman, there would be a Mercedes sports car wheelmarks right up the front of his shirt.

AVRIL VIRGO, on the probable aftermath of finding her snooker-playing husband John involved in an indiscretion

The one certain way for a woman to hold a man is to leave him for religion.

MURIEL SPARK

It is delightful to be a woman, but every man thanks the Lord devoutly that he isn't one.

OLIVE SCHREINER

WOMEN ON WOMEN

When a man of sixty runs off with a young woman I'm never surprised. I have a sneaking admiration for him. I wish him luck. After all, he's going to need it.

DEBORAH KERR

Behind almost every women you ever heard of stands a man who let her down.

NAOMI BLWEIN

How much does any woman need a man? A test tube full of sperm could be a dad.

FIONA PITT-KETHLEY

When I beat a man at pool, he seems to think he's had his willy chopped off.

SUE THOMPSON

Alas, why will a man spend months trying to hand over his liberty to a woman, and the rest of his life trying to get it back again?

HELEN ROWLAND

THE ART OF GENITAL PERSUASION

OUR POST-MODERN society, for better or worse, seems to have removed moral overtones from sex. The twin campaigns against sexual harassment in the workplace and molestation of minors have been stepped up in recent times, but when you're with a consenting adult you can do pretty much anything you like – so long as you don't wake the neighbours. Or frighten the horses . . .

Phyllis Diller and Zsa Zsa Gabor might strike you as being rather better experienced in this regard, but they both deny any such adventures. Gabor simply said she knew nothing about sex 'because I was always married', whereas, for Diller, 'Nothing happened in our boudoir. I nicknamed the water bed Lake Placid.'

Singer Linda Ronstadt says her big fantasy is to seduce a priest, which is laying it fairly bare. As far as Joan Rivers is concerned, 'The only time a woman ever has a true orgasm is when she's shopping. Every other time she's faking it.'

Jackie Collins believes it's all a matter of nationality.

'Continental people have sex lives,' she says, 'but the English have hot-water bottles.' Maybe – but is she the one to talk? On another occasion she said, 'Being happily married is thinking about sex.'

Zsa Zsa Gabor said 'Macho doesn't prove mucho', but I'll leave the last word on the subject to Mae West. In an attempt to explain what her unique attraction was, she said, 'It's not what I do but how I do it. It's not what I say but how I say it. And how I look when I'm saying it and doing it.'

It is said that change and a sense of humour are close to the heart of God. Could it be His ultimate joke that human beings – with all their aspirations to sophistication, higher intelligence and civilization – are at their happiest and most content naked, with legs splayed, with grunting heaving groaning faces distorted with the pleasure of love-making.

CATHY HOPKINS

Sex is good for slimming.

JULIA NEWMAR

Dirty dancing can be very satisfying. It's a form of safe sex.

JENNIFER GRAY

Nature abhors a virgin.

CLARE BOOTHE LUCE

THE ART OF GENITAL PERSUASION

Woody Allen was right when he said sex is only dirty if you're doing it the right way. It's not some sort of pristine, reverential ritual. You want reverent and pristine – go to church.

CYNTHIA HEIMEL

The best places to get to know girls are places where there's no urgency to score, places where you won't need witty chat-up lines. This includes the office, your college – or, if you're really desperate, the local embroidery class.

CATHY HOPKINS

He was a rather refined young man, who preferred sex dreams to visiting brothels, because he met a much nicer type of girl that way.

VIVIAN MERCER

Sex, to Peter Rachman, was like cleaning his teeth – and I was the toothpaste. It wasn't pleasant, it wasn't unpleasant. It was perfunctory, impersonal, and purely for his own pleasure. He never kissed and he never went down. He would arrive, and without ceremony take me roughly by the arm and push me in front of him towards the bedroom. I never saw his face while we had sex, as he always made me sit on top of him facing the other way. It did not concern him if the girl involved enjoyed herself or not – the feminist demand for orgasm that grew so vociferous in the sixties would probably have puzzled him, for all the emotion had been bludgeoned out of him in his early years as he fought for survival in Russian concentration camps.

CHRISTINE KEELER

My husband and I were looking at this questionnaire in the paper recently and I said to him, 'Are we married at all?' We didn't understand half the questions.

MEENA CRIBBENS

Dinner can be a strain on the first date. It implies sex, and unless both of you are very outgoing it is full of terrible pitfalls. Posh restaurants can make you feel a bit out of your depth. You're more likely to get pissed. And there's the hiatus after dinner of wondering what to do before bedtime. However, there is an outside chance, a very outside chance, that she might turn round to you at her front door and say, 'It's been a wonderful evening — would you like to come in and get laid?'

CATHY HOPKINS

People assume you slept your way to the top. Frankly, I couldn't sleep my way to the middle.

JONI EVANS

My best birth control now is to leave the lights on.

JOAN RIVERS

The reason I don't want to go to jail is because I'm afraid of lesbians.

ZSA ZSA GABOR

THE ART OF GENITAL PERSUASION

A 25-year-old virgin is like the man set upon by thieves – everyone passes by.

CHARLOTTE BINGHAM

I wish I had as much sex in bed as I get in the newspapers.

LINDA RONSTADT

If I had been caught making love to a male movie star at high noon in Times Square, it wouldn't even have made the six o'clock news. But Billie Jean and a woman . . .

BILLIE JEAN KING, on the scandal attendant on the public's discovery of her lesbianism

If sex is such a natural phenomenon, how come there are so many books on how to do it?

BETTE MIDLER

Q. Do you know the difference between a vaginal and clitoral orgasm?
A. No, but if you hum a few bars I'll try and fake it.

GRAFFITO

When you're a teenager trying to make it, you're terrified that your parents will walk in. But when you're trying to steal an amorous moment over forty, you're sure the *kids* will walk in, see the show and end up in therapy. As you can well imagine, it gets depressing dealing with all these trials and tribulations, and sometimes you'd prefer to stay home and have a meaningful relationship with your VCR.

WENDY DENNIS

WOMEN ON WOMEN

As I grow older and older
And totter towards the tomb
I find that I care less and less
Who goes to bed with whom.

DOROTHY L. SAYERS

Aren't women prudes if they don't — and prostitutes if they do?

KATE MILLETT

The next time I'm not just having an epidural for the birth — I'm having one for the conception as well.

SALLY JAMES

I have no sex appeal. I have to blindfold my vibrator.

JOAN RIVERS

A bisexual is a man who likes women as much as the next fellow.

ANON.

It's a silly question to ask a prostitute why she does it. They are the highest-paid professional women in America.

GAIL SHEEHY

All this talk about sex — big deal. The sun makes me happy. I eat a good fish and *that* makes me happy. I sleep with a good man, *he* makes me happy.

MELINA MERCOURI

THE ART OF GENITAL PERSUASION

Vasectomy means never having to say you're sorry.

ANON.

Being good in bed means I'm propped up with pillows and my mom brings me soup.

BROOKE SHIELDS

For many feminists, pornography is the theory and rape is the practice.

CHERIS KRAMARAE

A student undergoing a word-association test was asked why a snowstorm put him in mind of sex. He replied frankly: 'Because everything does.'

HONOR TRACY

The more sex becomes a non-issue in people's lives, the happier they are.

SHIRLEY MacLAINE

George Hamilton once told me to be a shrewd business-woman rather than a screwed actress.

JOAN COLLINS

There are lots of chicks who get laid by the director who *still* don't get the part.

CLAUDIA LINNEAR

It's been so long since I made love, I can't remember who gets tied up.

JOAN RIVERS

WOMEN ON WOMEN

If men could get pregnant, abortion would be a sacrament.

FLORYNCE KENNEDY

There are three secrets my mother told me: be a maid in the living room, a cook in the kitchen, and a whore in the bedroom. I figure as long as I have a maid and a cook, I'll do the rest myself.

JERRY HALL

A prude is someone who'll go so far and no fervour.

ANON.

Rape is the only crime in which the victim becomes the accused.

FREDA ADLER

For a woman, the first kiss is the end of the beginning. For a man, it's the beginning of the end.

HELEN ROWLAND

I consider promiscuity immoral. Not because sex is evil, but rather because it's too good and too important.

AYN RAND

You cannot decree that women should be sexually free when they're not economically free.

SHERE HITE

Sex is like washing your face. You do it because you have to.

SOPHIA LOREN

THE ART OF GENITAL PERSUASION

It's a bad thing because it rumples the bedclothes.

JACQUELINE KENNEDY ONASSIS

We're living in an age where it's the *men* who say, 'Not tonight darling, I have a headache.'

OPRAH WINFREY

Some girls shrink from sex; others get bigger and bigger.

ANON.

Is sexual harassment a problem for the self-employed?

VICTORIA WOOD

Sex is God's biggest joke on human beings.

BETTE DAVIS

When the cat's away, it's probably mating.

EVA GABOR

Life is a sexually transmitted disease.

ANON.

These are immensely trying times for men and women, and I've learned that only a sense of humour will get you through. A man I know said recently, 'I'm having sex with myself a lot these days.' When I asked solicitously how he was coping through the drought, he quipped: 'Oh well, I smoke two cigarettes and ask myself, "Was it good for you?" '

WENDY DENNIS

37

WOMEN ON WOMEN

They say disarm all rapists — but it's not their arms I'm worried about.

JOAN RIVERS

If they had as much adultery going on in New York as they said in the divorce courts, they'd never have a chance to make the beds at the Plaza.

ZSA ZSA GABOR

Sex is bad for one — but good for two.

ANON.

Catherine the great ruled 30 million people and had 3,000 lovers. I do the best I can in two hours.

MAE WEST, commenting on her role in her revue
Catherine was Great

Sex is a baffling thing when it doesn't happen. I used to wake up in the morning when I was married, and wonder if the whole world was crazy, whooping about sex all the time. It was like hearing all the time that stove polish was the greatest invention on earth.

MARILYN MONROE

Permissiveness is merely removing the dust sheets from our follies.

EDNA O'BRIEN

Celibacy isn't an inherited characteristic.

ANON.

THE ART OF GENITAL PERSUASION

All heterosexual men, whether monogamous or not, fantasize about sex with other women, so that even if they are monogamous in *fact*, they're unfaithful countless times in their reveries.

CAROL BOTWIN

Before we go through sexual ecstasy, we have to go through sexual abasement.

EDNA O'BRIEN

I think sex is better than logic, but I can't prove it.

ANON.

Spinster means you're old and frustrated and unattractive and wear your hair in a bun and have too many cats and probably knit. The worst that can be said of a bachelor is that he's probably gay.

CYNTHIA HEIMEL

The Women's Movement hasn't changed my sex life at all – it wouldn't dare.

ZSA ZSA GABOR

A girl who knows all the answers is often asked something that's completely out of the question.

ANON.

Physical love, forbidden as it was twenty or thirty years ago, has now become boringly obligatory.

FRANÇOISE SAGAN

WOMEN ON WOMEN

You know more about a man in one night in bed than you do in months of conversation. In the sack, they can't cheat.

EDITH PIAF

Among men, sex sometimes results in intimacy; among women, intimacy sometimes results in sex.

BARBARA CARTLAND

Sex is 90 per cent in the head.

GERMAINE GREER

David used sex the way a cat sprays, to mark his territory.

ANGELA BOWIE, on her famous ex-husband

Any girl who swears no man has ever made love to her has a right to swear.

SOPHIA LOREN

There are a lot of more interesting things in life than sex. Gardening, for instance.

JEAN ALEXANDER

Men have somehow calculated that it's safer to have sex with someone than to get in an aeroplane, or cross a traffic-filled street.

CAROL BOTWIN

Promiscuity is, if anything, a stepping stone to love.

EDNA O'BRIEN

THE ART OF GENITAL PERSUASION

A lady is one who never shows her underwear unintentionally.

LILLIAN DAY

Much more genius is needed to make love than to command armies.

NINON DE LENCLOS

Europeans used to say Americans were puritanical. Then they discovered that we weren't, so now they say we're obsessed with sex.

MARY McCARTHY

Robert Benchley and I had an office so tiny that an inch smaller and it would have been adultery.

DOROTHY PARKER

France is the only place where you can make love in the afternoon without people hammering on your door.

BARBARA CARTLAND

Sex has become such a loaded gun these days that sex on the first date all too often turns out to be sex on the last date.

WENDY DENNIS

For all the pseudo-sophistication of twentieth-century theory, it's still assumed that a man should make love as if his principal intention was to people the wilderness.

GERMAINE GREER

WOMEN ON WOMEN

The sexual ideology of current feminism is reactionary, repressive and puritanical.

CAMILLE PAGLIA

When a husband leaves his wife, everyone automatically assumes it's for pure sex. But when a woman leaves her husband, it's rare for people to think that. Women don't leave for sex – they're too clever for that.

SHIRLEY ESKAPA

How do girls get minks? The same way minks get minks.

GRAFFITO

The only reason I would take up jogging is so I could hear heavy breathing again.

ERMA BOMBECK

WHAT MAKES ME TICK

NOT EVERYONE in the public eye has an ego the size of Trump Towers. Did you know that Linda Ronstadt once said: 'There are times I've prayed for a bus to hit me so I'd have an excuse not to perform'?

Acting has been dubbed the Shy Person's Revenge. How often is a life in the limelight an attempt to overcompensate for deep-seated bashfulness or diffidence? And how many people who thrive on the smell of the greasepaint and the roar of the crowd are shivering jellies when the curtains come down?

Many of the celebrities featured in the following pages suffer from (enjoy?) I-strain; many more seem to inhabit the limbo between genius and insanity, that schizoid twilight zone that is the fool's gold at the end of the starstruck rainbow. What they have in common is a frank, upfront, in-your-face form of expression. Their revelations should help to demythologize them in our eyes, and help us realize we're all equally vulnerable, equally idiosyncratic, equally infuriating . . . and equally *real*. Whether we're making love to 25,000 people, like Janis Joplin, and then going home alone – or, like Judy Garland in the autumn of her career, desperately waiting for the phone to ring with an offer she couldn't refuse.

I'm a mad Amazon, a drag queen, an opera diva. I'm too much, too loud, too fast, too theatrical for America.

CAMILLE PAGLIA

People think I'm something the media created. The fact is that twenty-six years ago there was this scrunched-up little pink baby named Julia Roberts. I'm a girl like anybody else.

JULIA ROBERTS

I'm one of those people who just can't help getting a kick out of life – even if it's a kick in the teeth.

POLLY ADLER

If I knew what I was so anxious about, I wouldn't be so anxious.

MIGNON McLAUGHLIN

I've been so lonely for long periods in my life that if a rat walked in, I would have welcomed it.

LOUISE NEVELSON

WHAT MAKES ME TICK

When I was born, I was so surprised I didn't talk for a year and a half.

GRACIE ALLEN

I have this *gay guy* way of looking at things.

CAMILLE PAGLIA

I was a personality before I became a person.

BARBRA STREISAND

I can hold a note as long as the Chase Manhattan Bank.

ETHEL MERMAN

I liked myself better when I wasn't me.

CAROL BURNETT

Perhaps the thing I might do best is to be a long-distance lorry driver.

PRINCESS ANNE

Every night I make love to 25,000 people on stage and go home alone.

JANIS JOPLIN

I'm an actor. An actress is someone who wears feather boas.

SIGOURNEY WEAVER

I started as a dumb blonde whore; I'll end as one.

MARILYN MONROE

I have my standards. They may be low, but I have them.
BETTE MIDLER

I'm an Irish Catholic so I have a long iceberg of guilt.
EDNA O'BRIEN

I never go out unless I look like Joan Crawford the movie star. If you want to see the girl next door – go next door.
JOAN CRAWFORD

I didn't throw myself off my balcony only because I knew people would photograph me dead.
BRIGITTE BARDOT

If I believed everything I read about myself, I'd hate my guts too.
ZSA ZSA GABOR

Nobody can be exciting like me. Sometimes I even have trouble doing it myself.
TALLULAH BANKHEAD

I'm very patient, provided I get my own way in the end.
MARGARET THATCHER

If I'm such a legend, then why am I so lonely? If I'm such a legend, why do I sit at home for hours staring at the darned telephone, hoping it's out of order?
JUDY GARLAND

WHAT MAKES ME TICK

I am troubled. I'm dissatisfied. I'm Irish.

MARIANNE MOORE

I've never been very good at being a member of any group
– other than a group of two, that is.

MARILYN MONROE

I shaved my head because I was bored.

SINEAD O'CONNOR

I'm neither a movie star nor a singer these days – more
an inflated swimsuit.

SAMANTHA FOX

I do a lot of dumb things – but men like that.

KYLIE MINOGUE

I'm only old-fashioned from the waist up.

CHARLOTTE RAMPLING

I identify with the strength of Frances Farmer, the weakness of Vivien Leigh, the loneliness of Judy Garland . . .
and the attitude of Don Corleone.

WENDY JAMES

I'm basically an old tart. I'd be happy just doing com-
mercials.

JULIE WALTERS

WOMEN ON WOMEN

I always wanted to be a nun, but when I discovered boys were out of bounds, I got cold feet.

MADONNA

If I'd been a ranch, they'd have named me Bar Nothing.

RITA HAYWORTH

There was a rumour that I used to be male and had a sex change. That's not a bad rumour.

ANNIE LENNOX

I'm still not sure whether I'm a staggeringly extroverted latent introvert or an irritatingly introverted latent extrovert.

SANDIE SHAW

I generally avoid temptation, unless I can't resist it.

MAE WEST

They still pray for me in the convent.

EDNA O'BRIEN

Ultimately I want to be the purest creature in the world.

SINEAD O'CONNOR

Dancing on my mother's grave was an attempt to accept her death.

MADONNA

WHAT MAKES ME TICK

People are used to looking at me as if I were a kind of mirror instead of a person. They don't see me, they see their own hidden thoughts – and then they whitewash themselves by claiming I embody these secret thoughts.

MARILYN MONROE

I was out of the world called Normal for a very long time, and occasionally I slip back even now. I know I have a job to do, though, and it's this: to attempt to break every social norm, turn it back on itself and see that it is laughed at.

ROSEANNE

There are so many things locked up in my head, I feel that if there was a can opener that could open my brain, all these feelings would gush out like some unstoppable water tap.

JUDY GARLAND

There are times when I feel so close to the edge I could just tip over.

JESSICA LANGE

I'm an inkblot. People see what they want to see in me.

GOLDIE HAWN

Outside I look OK, but deep down I'm a definite basket case.

BARBRA STREISAND

I cry when I see *The Wizard of Oz*. Every time.

MADONNA

I'm a witch with acute extrasensory perception, eerie pre-
monitions and haunting superstitions. Never a day of my
life goes by but I wear red to keep the demons at bay.

SOPHIA LOREN

I guess I still think getting paid to sing is too good to
be true. And if it ends tomorrow, I can always go back
to doing hair.

TAMMY WYNETTE

Some people go skiing in the Bahamas; I'm comforted by
pasta.

OPRAH WINFREY

Before I went into analysis I told everyone lies. But when
you spend all that money, you start to come clean.

JANE FONDA

So many times I drive around in my expensive car and
just think, 'God, I'm just a gal from Michigan.'

MADONNA

I hung on to a thread of sanity as hordes of women decided
that feminism meant they should turn themselves into
small men and wear pinstriped suits and bow ties and
pursue the key to the executive washroom as if it were
the holy grail.

CYNTHIA HEIMEL

WHAT MAKES ME TICK

Three highballs and I think I'm St Francis of Assisi.
DOROTHY PARKER

To put it bluntly, I seem to be a whole superstructure without the foundation. But I'm working on the foundation.

MARILYN MONROE

I am a child that's been abused, so any time I do anything, that's at the back of it. That's the only reason I've ever sung and it's what's kept me alive.

SINEAD O'CONNOR

I don't mind how much my ministers talk – as long as they do what I say.

MARGARET THATCHER

I grew up in the back end of celebrity. My parents had peaked when I was born, so it was downhill after that.

CARRIE FISHER

I am ashamed of confessing that I have nothing to confess.
FRANNY BURNEY

I'm just another working mum.

JOAN COLLINS

I have been one of the great lovers of my century.
SARAH BERNHARDT

WOMEN ON WOMEN

I'm a big star and I can't even get laid.

JANIS JOPLIN

My ultimate goal is to become a saint.

MARISA BERENSON

I postpone death by living, by suffering, by error, by risking, by giving, by losing.

ANAÏS NIN

If I stopped moving I'd probably explode.

MADONNA

Even when I was six years of age I was extraordinarily aggressive and enjoyed competition and combat. My father taught me to put up my fists and defend myself like a man, and throughout my life I have done that many times when people angered me, offended me or just plain refused to get out of my way.

CAMILLE PAGLIA

I don't want to get to the end of my life and find that I just lived the length of it. I want to have lived the width of it as well.

DIANE ACKERMAN

Flops are part of my life's menu, and I've never been a girl to miss out on any of the courses.

ROSALIND RUSSELL

WHAT MAKES ME TICK

I worry about scientists discovering that lettuce has been fattening all along.

ERMA BOMBECK

I have often wished I had time to cultivate modesty, but I am too busy thinking about myself.

EMMYLOU HARRIS

I am ugly, I am stupid. What will become of me? Who am I? What right do I have to be alive? I am a hollow, empty, very superficial thing; I'll never amount to anything.

DR RUTH WESTHEIMER, in a diary entry before she became a world-famous sex therapist

It's a funny thing about happiness . . . it just sort of sneaks up on you. Some days I feel happy because of the way the light strikes things. Or for some beautifully immature reason like finding myself running to the kitchen to make some *toast*.

JONI MITCHELL

I enjoy sleeping with men, but only fall in love with women.

CAMILLE PAGLIA

I can't stand to sing the same song the same way two nights in succession. If you can, then it ain't music, it's close order drill, or exercise, or yodelling, or something – not music.

BILLIE HOLIDAY

I signed myself into the Betty Ford Clinic because I was sick and tired of feeling sick and tired.

LIZA MINNELLI

Broadway has been very good to me – but then I've been very good to Broadway.

ETHEL MERMAN

I want to be the girl in *Indiana Jones*. I would love to do an adventure movie where I was saving the world.

ROSEANNE

I'd rather have roses on my table than diamonds on my neck.

EMMA GOLDMAN

Most people who are as attractive, witty and intelligent as I am are usually conceited.

JOAN RIVERS

My ambition? To rule the world.

MADONNA

I have three phobias which, could I mute them, would make my life as slick as a sonnet but as dull as ditchwater: I hate to go to bed, I hate to get up, and I hate to be alone.

TALLULAH BANKHEAD

WHAT MAKES ME TICK

I've been told that nobody sings the word 'hunger' like I do.

BILLIE HOLIDAY

I believe in the total depravity of inanimate things. The elusiveness of soap, the knottiness of string, the transitory nature of buttons, the inclination of suspenders to twist, and of hooks to forsake their lawful eyes and cleave only unto the hairs of their hapless owner's head.

KATHERINE ASHLEY

I miss the animal buoyancy of New York, the animal vitality. I did not mind that it had no meaning and no depth.

ANAÏS NIN

There are two actions that are reprehensible to me. One is the act of beginning a sentence and then refusing to finish it. The other is murder.

LUCILLE KALLEN

My mission in life is to save feminism from the feminists.

CAMILLE PAGLIA

I am thirty, but there are things about me that are still fifteen. I love to love and I hate to leave, but I love freely and I leave freely.

BRIGITTE BARDOT

I'm never going to be famous. My name will never be writ large on the roster of Those Who Do Things. I don't do anything. Not a single thing. I used to bite my nails, but I don't even do that any more.

DOROTHY PARKER

People think because I'm in television I have this great social life. Let me tell you, I can count on my fingers the number of dates I've had in four years I've been in Baltimore – and that includes the ones I've paid for.

OPRAH WINFREY

I'm a real librarian at heart – very shy.

BETTE MIDLER

Oh God – how I wish I were Liza Minnelli.

RAQUEL WELCH

If I were a teenager today, I'd probably be a pink-haired punk.

MARY WHITEHOUSE

I enjoy reading biographies because I want to know about people who messed up the world.

MARIE DRESSLER

I aspire to be terrifically boring.

JODIE FOSTER

WHAT MAKES ME TICK

I have been very rich, very beautiful, much adulated, very famous . . . and very unhappy.

BRIGITTE BARDOT

I love wild, crazy, wonderful sex – but I also love romance. I don't jump on every man who comes into view.

KIM BASINGER

Every man I've ever been attracted to has been known as a ladies man. I like men who love women.

JESSICA LANGE

I've never kept anything in life without wishing I had given it away, or given anything away without wishing I had kept it.

LOUISE BROOKS

When I appear in public, people expect me to neigh, grind my teeth, paw the ground and swish my tail – none of which is easy.

PRINCESS ANNE

You get more by doing what comes naturally than you do by 'efforting' to get things. I move with the flow and take life's cues. Let the universe handle the details.

OPRAH WINFREY

I'm not just involved in tennis, I'm *committed* to it. Do you know the difference? Think of ham and eggs. The chicken is involved, the pig is committed.

MARTINA NAVRATILOVA

What a wonderful life I've had – I only wish I'd realized it sooner.

COLETTE

What annoys me most? Unused fireplaces, sweet peas, badly made beds – and Miriam Hopkins.

BETTE DAVIS

Myself and I are on the best of terms.

IVY COMPTON-BURNETT

I'm the impatient type. If I want to take a photograph of a flower, I'm not going to wait for it to open. In fact I'm probably going to bring the sun over to it.

MARTINA NAVRATILOVA

Ask Nureyev to stop dancing, ask Sinatra to stop singing – then you can ask me to stop playing tennis.

BILLIE JEAN KING

They say I'm outspoken – but not by many.

SHELLEY WINTERS

I'm just a girl who runs.

ZOLA BUDD

I'm a very soft person. I'm not aggressive; I'm very feminine. I worry, I cry, I get premenstrual tension. I don't wake up every morning saying: I'm going to be a troublemaker today.

SINEAD O'CONNOR

WHAT MAKES ME TICK

I want to be syndicated in every city known to mankind.

OPRAH WINFREY

Even when I was a little girl I knew I wanted the whole world to know who I was, to love me and be affected by me.

MADONNA

I think I think too much. That's why I drink.

JANIS JOPLIN

The Jews have produced only three original geniuses: Christ, Spinoza and myself.

GERTRUDE STEIN

I do not want people to be very agreeable, as it saves me the trouble of liking them a great deal.

JANE AUSTEN

I want to be left alone.

GRETA GARBO

It takes a lot of time to be a genius. You have to sit around so much doing nothing.

GERTRUDE STEIN

I should like to be a horse.

QUEEN ELIZABETH I, as a child

I used to pick my navel until it bled.

MARIETTE HARTLEY

WOMEN ON WOMEN

I am one of those who never knows the direction of my journey until I have almost arrived.

ANNA LOUISE STRONG

I live with the people I create. It has always made my essential loneliness less keen.

CARSON McCULLERS

I am really only myself when I'm somebody else whom I have endowed with these wonderful qualities from my imagination.

ZELDA FITZGERALD

I wasn't allowed to speak while my husband was alive, and since he's gone no one has been able to shut me up.

HEDDA HOPPER

I never sleep when I am over-happy, over-unhappy – or in bed with a strange man.

EDNA O'BRIEN

FAME AND MISFORTUNE

WHEN PEOPLE become famous, they tend to look on it as an upward curve stretching to infinity. When the inevitable fall comes, they're not so much depressed as befuddled.

If the lives – or rather premature deaths – of Judy Garland and her like are anything to go by, those who attain success are usually the ones most ill-equipped to handle it. One thing is sure, though: when you reach the top of the rollercoaster, your days of living ordinarily are numbered. And the higher up you go, the more vertiginous your perch. The people who put you up there are also going to be first in the queue to tear you down again.

There are very few things in life more fickle than success – particularly overnight success. And overnight success, as we know, can take up to fifty years to happen. Or not happen. The dictates of showbusiness – if not mathematics – would also seem to account for the fact that Performer A's success accelerates Performer B's decline, almost by default.

The main problem with those who are struck by fame

is the fact that they're less able to handle anonymity than those who've never had anything else. After being a somebody it's all the more difficult being a nobody again. It's even worse for people who *started* at the top. They tend to become shooting stars – in all senses.

The last word should go to Rosemary Clooney, who remarked: 'In the final analysis, it's true that fame is unimportant. No matter how great a man is, the size of his funeral usually depends on the weather.'

To be content with little is hard. To be content with much – impossible.

MARIE VAN EBNER ESCHENBACH

The penalty for success is to be bored by the attentions of people who formerly snubbed you.

MARY WILSON LITTLE

If you stay away from parties, you're called a snob. If you go, you're called an exhibitionist. If you don't talk, you're dumb. If you do talk, you're quarrelsome. You can't win with fame. So excuse me while I change my nail polish . . .

LANA TURNER

You can't get spoiled if you do your own ironing.

MERYL STREEP

Behind every successful man stands an amazed woman.

MARYON PEARSON

FAME AND MISFORTUNE

There's only one real sin, and that's to persuade yourself that the second best is anything *but* second best.

DORIS LESSING

Too often the opportunity knocks, but by the time you push back the chain, unlock the two locks and shut off the burglar alarm – it's too late.

RITA COOLIDGE

For a while there it was either me or the Ayatollah on the covers of the national magazines.

MERYL STREEP

Fame always brings loneliness. Success is as ice-cold and lonely as the North Pole.

VICKI BAUM

It is good to have an end to journey towards, but it is the journey that matters, in the end.

URSULA LEGUIN

Success, to me, is having ten honeydew melons and eating only the top half of each one.

BARBRA STREISAND

To gain that which is worth having, it may be necessary to lose everything else.

BERNADETTE McALISKEY

I've got two reasons for success, and I'm standing on both of them.

BETTY GRABLE

Success is counted sweetest by those who ne'er succeed.

EMILY DICKINSON

Fame for me means being able to torture a higher class of man than I used to.

SHARON STONE

By the time you've found the key to success, they've changed the lock.

ANON.

Everybody always asks me, 'How does it feel to make a comeback?' Which is really strange, because I never really know where I've been.

JUDY GARLAND

Fame is like winning the Donkey Derby. For a couple of days you think, God, I'm on the cover of *Rolling Stone* . . . then you forget it.

ANNIE LENNOX

I don't want to be an icon, particularly. I've already been there and got the T-shirt.

SANDIE SHAW

FAME AND MISFORTUNE

I feel as though it's all happening to someone right next to me. I'm close, I can feel it, I can hear it, but it isn't really me.

MARILYN MONROE

I became famous because I wanted to be loved.

MADONNA

People used to hate me and now they love me. Not that I give a damn either way.

CHER

Being famous is lonely because you can't trust people.

SINEAD O'CONNOR

You haven't made it until they call you difficult.

DIANA ROSS

I climbed the ladder of success wrong by wrong.

MAE WEST

Success has killed more men than bullets.

TEXAS GUINAN

You can't understand being hugely famous until it happens . . . and then it's too late to decide if you want it or not.

MADONNA

There's nothing better than to know I can be taking a bath at home and at the same time someone is watching me in Brazil.

BARBRA STREISAND

You can only buy so many towels.

OPRAH WINFREY

I can't even go out with somebody nice these days. I always feel they're dating me not because they like me but because I'm Sinead O'Connor.

SINEAD O'CONNOR

Sometimes I have this vision that I'd like to walk down the street naked and leave it all behind.

KIM BASINGER

I don't want just the roar of the Benzedrine, the smell of the crowd and some clammy little coffee bar to call home. I want the fucking world.

ANGELA BOWIE

I never looked through a keyhole without finding someone was looking back.

JUDY GARLAND

The fact that I became famous gives me a form of happiness, but it's only temporary. It's like caviar: it's nice, but I don't want caviar every night.

MARILYN MONROE

FAME AND MISFORTUNE

A girl is a girl; it's nice to be told you're successful at it.

RITA HAYWORTH

All they ever did for me at MGM was change my leading men and the water in my swimming pool.

ESTHER WILLIAMS

The worst part of success is trying to find someone who's happy for you.

ANN SHERIDAN

Success in showbusiness depends on your ability to make – and keep – friends.

SOPHIA TUCKER

I find it's as hard to live down an early triumph as an early indiscretion.

EDNA ST VINCENT MILLAY

If at first you don't succeed – you're fired.

JEAN GRAMAN

THE WRITE STUFF

THERE WAS a time when the representation of female scribes on our book (and even magazine) shelves smacked of tokenism. No more. Virginia Woolf's comment that a woman called 'Anon.' might well have written many of the anthologized poems of yesteryear could be true, but we have left our Currer Bells and George Eliots behind us. Today, women can stand up and be counted among the literati – if not the glitterati. Putting pen to paper, and being the acknowledged author of the work in question, is a small but important step on the march towards sexual equality.

How do women feel about what they write, though? How do they prepare for their exertions? Who do they write for? And what if it comes out wrong? Men, the cliché goes, write from the head, and women from the heart. The truth of the matter is that all writing comes from the head, heart and soul intermixed. There might also be some blood, sweat and tears.

❦

68

THE WRITE STUFF

Writing is so difficult that I often feel that writers, having had their hell on earth, will escape all punishment thereafter.

JESSAMYN WEST

I shall live badly if I do not write, and I shall write badly if I do not live.

FRANÇOISE SAGAN

How can I know what I think unless I see what I write?

ERICA JONG

Anyone who's going to be a writer already knows enough at fifteen to write several novels.

MAY SARTON

I'm constantly writing autobiography, but I have to turn it into fiction in order to give it credibility.

KATHERINE PATERSON

The best time for planning a book is when you're doing the dishes.

AGATHA CHRISTIE

Perversity is the muse of modern literature.

SUSAN SONTAG

I believe all literature started as gossip.

RITA MAE BROWN

WOMEN ON WOMEN

If you have a burning restless urge to write or paint, simply eat something sweet and the feeling will pass.

FRAN LEBOWITZ

Surely there's enough unhappiness in life without having to go to books for it.

DOROTHY PARKER

I've always believed in writing without a collaborator, because where two people are writing the same book, each believes he gets all the worries and only half the royalties.

AGATHA CHRISTIE

Only in romantic novels are the beautiful guaranteed happiness.

CYNTHIA ASQUITH

All autobiographies are alibi-ographies.

CLARE BOOTHE LUCE

Readers are plentiful, thinkers are rare.

HARRIET MARTINEAU

I have only read one book in my life, and that is *White Fang*. It's so frightfully good, I've never bothered to read another.

NANCY MITFORD

A great many people now reading and writing would be better employed in keeping rabbits.

DAME EDITH SITWELL

THE WRITE STUFF

A person who publishes a book wilfully appears in public with his pants down.

EDNA ST VINCENT MILLAY

Everywhere I go, I'm asked if I think the university stifles writers. My opinion is that they don't stifle enough of them.

FLANNERY O'CONNOR

I don't want to do book reviewing any more. It cuts in on my reading too much.

DOROTHY PARKER

Literature is strewn with the wreckage of men who have minded beyond reason the opinions of others.

VIRGINIA WOOLF

If I had to give young writers advice, I would say: don't listen to writers' advice.

LILLIAN HELLMAN

The old reliable cup of tea is all I need to get started.

EDNA O'BRIEN, on her powers of motivation

Writing is like getting married. One should never commit oneself until one is amazed at one's luck.

IRIS MURDOCH

Never judge a cover by its book.

FRAN LEBOWITZ

Writers long for the absence of hypocrisy: a naked, visceral, bleeding truth. It occupies a place in the psyche that religion *should*.

EDNA O'BRIEN

I hang my laundry on the line when I write.

JONI MITCHELL

One writer I know has the unnerving habit of taking two extra copies of all his love letters — one for himself and the other for the British Museum.

JILLY COOPER

I've only spent about 10 per cent of my energies on writing. The other 90 per cent went on keeping my head above water.

KATHERINE ANNE PORTER

If I'm a lousy writer, a helluva lot of people have lousy taste.

GRACE METALIOUS

Writers should be read, but neither seen nor heard.

DAPHNE DU MAURIER

I'd like to have money and I'd like to be a good writer. These two *can* come together and I hope they will, but if that's too adorable . . . I'll take the money.

DOROTHY PARKER

THE WRITE STUFF

Nothing stinks like a pile of unpublished writing.

SYLVIA PLATH

When I'm near the end of a book I sleep in the same room with it. Somehow the book doesn't leave you when you sleep right next to it.

JOAN DIDION

I can't write five words without changing seven.

DOROTHY PARKER

Most writers had unhappy childhoods.

JUDITH KRANTZ

For me, poetry is an evasion of the real job of writing prose.

SYLVIA PLATH

One handles truths like dynamite. Literature is one vast hypocrisy, a giant deception. All writers have concealed more than they revealed.

ANAÏS NIN

Books succeed . . . and lives fail.

ELIZABETH BARRETT BROWNING

Literature is the next best thing to God.

EDNA O'BRIEN

Creative literature that is unconcerned with sex is inconceivable.

GERTRUDE STEIN

All books are either dreams or swords.

AMY LOWELL

The poet is neither an intellectual nor an emotional being alone. He feels his thoughts and thinks his sensations.

ELIZABETH DREW

I was never allowed to read the popular American children's books of my day because, as my mother said, the children spoke bad English without the author's knowing it.

EDITH WHARTON

Writing is the diametric opposite of having fun. All of life, as far as I'm concerned, is an excuse not to write. I just write when fear overtakes me. It's really scary just getting to the desk. We're talking five hours here – my mouth goes dry, my heart beats fast: I react psychologically the way other people do when the plane loses an engine.

FRAN LEBOWITZ

I'm not happy when I'm writing, but I'm more unhappy when I'm not.

FRANNIE HURST

THE WRITE STUFF

I have a superstition that if I talk about plot, it's like letting sand out of a hole in the bottom of a bag.

SHIRLEY HAZZARD

I don't have a clear idea of who my characters are until they start talking.

JOAN DIDION

The original writer, as long as he isn't dead, is always scandalous.

SIMONE DE BEAUVOIR

Nothing you write, if you hope to be any good, ever comes out as you first hoped.

LILLIAN HELLMAN

Writing keeps me from believing everything I read.

GLORIA STEINEM

I am not afraid the book will be controversial. I'm afraid it will *not* be controversial.

FLANNERY O'CONNOR

Writers talk too much.

LILLIAN HELLMAN

Life resembles a novel more often than a novel resembles life.

GEORGE SAND

WOMEN ON WOMEN

If it makes my whole body so cold no fire can warm me, I know it's poetry.

EMILY DICKINSON

Better to write twaddle, anything, than nothing at all.

KATHARINE MANSFIELD

I think I may boast myself to be, with all possible vanity, the most unlearned and uninformed female who ever dared to be an authoress.

JANE AUSTEN

It does no harm to repeat, as often as you can, 'Without me, the literary industry would not exist.'

DORIS LESSING

Writing is a trade which is learned by writing.

SIMONE DE BEAUVOIR

Books are funny little portable pieces of thought.

SUSAN SONTAG

Remarks are not literature.

GERTRUDE STEIN

A poem on a flea may be a very good poem, and a poem on the immortality of the soul may be a very bad poem.

ELIZABETH DREW

THE WRITE STUFF

I have decided to be a poet. My father says there isn't a suitable career structure for poets, and no pensions and other boring things, but I am quite decided.

SUE TOWNSEND

When people, women included, hear that you are writing, they assume that it is simply a hobby to fill in time between doing the washing-up and the ironing. It couldn't possibly be a profession.

RACHEL BILLINGTON

Contrary to what many of you might imagine, a career in letters is not without its drawbacks – chief among them the unpleasant fact that one is frequently called upon to sit down and write.

FRAN LEBOWITZ

If one were blissfully happy, one wouldn't have to write.

EDNA O'BRIEN

The art of writing is the art of applying the seat of the pants to the seat of the chair.

MARY HEATON

I find I always have to write something on a steamed mirror.

ELAINE DUNDY

Besides Shakespeare and me, who do you think there is?

GERTRUDE STEIN

WOMEN ON WOMEN

Some say life is the thing, but I prefer reading.

RUTH RENDELL

An autobiography is a book that proves that the only thing wrong with the author is his memory.

EVE POLLARD

Hiring someone to write your autobiography is like paying someone to take a bath for you.

MAE WEST

You should always believe all you read in the newspapers, as this makes them more interesting.

ROSE MACAULAY

Lunacy is the foundation of all writing.

EDNA O'BRIEN

The writer who loses his self-doubt should stop writing immediately. The time has come for him to lay aside his pen.

COLETTE

Magazines all too frequently lead to books and should be regarded as the heavy petting of literature.

FRAN LEBOWITZ

My writing is a hollow and failing substitute for real feeling.

VIRGINIA WOOLF

THE WRITE STUFF

Every book is like a purge. At the end of it, one is empty, like a dry shell on the beach waiting for the tide to come in again.

DAPHNE DU MAURIER

I am a corpse who moves a pen that writes. I am a vessel for a voice that echoes. I write a novel and annihilate whole forests. I rearrange the cosmos inch by inch.

ERICA JONG

Nothing induces me to read a novel except when I have to make money by writing about it. I detest them.

VIRGINIA WOOLF

BEAUTY IS ONLY SIN DEEP

'MY FACE was always so made up,' confessed Shelley Winters, 'it looked like it had the decorators in.' Not a few people believe that Joan Collins has had so many face-lifts that when she answers the phone these days she has to put the receiver on her *forehead*.

There are *paparazzi* who will tell you that Marilyn Monroe never looked as good in the flesh as she did on celluloid – because the camera loved her. And as far as Mel Gibson is concerned, 'The most beautiful women in the world can look like dogshit on camera – though, fortunately for me, it also works the other way round.'

Can an actress make it big in the movie world today if she hasn't been blessed with *Vogue*-style looks? Jane Fonda is in no doubt about why *she* made it to the top. 'I'm perfect,' she said some time ago. 'The areas I need help on aren't negotiable. They're to do with gravity.'

There's nothing like believing in yourself, Jane, but I prefer Joan Rivers' comment: 'Jane didn't get that terrific body from exercise; she got it from lifting all that money.'

The reason I come off as being sexy and attractive is because I've had myself rebuilt. I had the hair under my arms taken care of, and I had an operation to firm up my breasts. I also spend about $1,000 a week to have my toenails, fingernails, eyebrows and hair put in top shape. I'm the female equivalent of a counterfeit $20 bill. Half of what you see is a pretty good reproduction . . . and the rest is fraud.

CHER

In my next life, I'd like to come back five feet two inches – and the best ass and tits you've ever seen.

ANDIE MacDOWELL

The only parts left of my original body are my elbows.

PHYLLIS DILLER

The only reason my feet are so small is because things don't grow well in the shade.

DOLLY PARTON

In my own mind, I'm still a fat brunette from Toledo – and I always will be.

GLORIA STEINEM

I've always looked better lying down.

JERRY HALL

WOMEN ON WOMEN

We have antenatal treatment and we have postnatal treatment — but we still have these appalling figures.

ELEANOR RATHBONE

When I go to the beauty parlour, I always use the emergency entrance. Sometimes I just go for an *estimate*.

PHYLLIS DILLER

When I was born I was so ugly the doctor slapped the afterbirth.

JOAN RIVERS

It's easy for a girl to stay on the straight and narrow if she's built that way.

ZSA ZSA GABOR

Glamour is what makes a man ask you for your phone number — but what also makes a woman ask for the name of your tailor.

LILLY DECK

If God had to give women wrinkles, He might at least have put them on the soles of their feet.

NINON DE LENCLOS

I don't like to get a suntan because I like to feel blonde all over.

MARILYN MONROE

Everything you see I owe to spaghetti.

SOPHIA LOREN

BEAUTY IS ONLY SIN DEEP

Woman's chains have been forged by men, not by anatomy.

ESTELLE RAMEY

My body is so bad, a Peeping Tom looked in the window and pulled the blinds down.

JOAN RIVERS

The art of managing a man has to be learned from birth. It depends to some extent on the distribution of one's curves.

MARY HYDE

Love can't last around poverty – and neither can a woman's looks.

KRISTIN HUNTER

Elegance has a bad effect on my constitution.

LOUISA MAY ALCOTT

My photographs don't do me justice – they look just like me.

PHYLLIS DILLER

I never forget that a woman's first job is to choose the right shade of lipstick.

CAROLE LOMBARD

A curved line is the loveliest distance between two points.

MAE WEST

WOMEN ON WOMEN

Men look *at* themselves in mirrors; women look *for* themselves.

ELISSA MELAMED

I look like a duck. It's the way my mouth sort of curls up, or my nose tilts. I should have played Howard the Duck.

MICHELLE PFEIFFER

I hate my gummy smile.

JULIA ROBERTS

I've always been a beanpole.

DARYL HANNAH

My breasts? They're just round things with brown bits on the end that I hit my chin off when I run for the bus.

SAMANTHA FOX

A homely face and no figure have aided many women heavenward.

MINNA ANTRIM

Everyone's just laughing at me. Big breasts, big ass, big deal.

MARILYN MONROE

All my life until now, people thought me unattractive. Now they don't . . . but it's too late for me to do anything about it.

CHER

BEAUTY IS ONLY SIN DEEP

How long does it take me to do my hair? I don't know —
I'm never there.

DOLLY PARTON

It's an ill wind that blows after you've been to the hairdresser.

ANON.

At the moment I don't believe in plastic surgery, but
when I'm an old broad maybe I'll change my mind and
say, 'Doc, lift everything thirty feet!'

MICHELLE PFEIFFER

The problem with beauty is that it's like being born rich
and getting progressively poorer.

JOAN COLLINS

When I wake up in the morning and look in the mirror,
I realize that one of the reasons I don't have a handgun is
that I would have shot my thighs off years ago.

OPRAH WINFREY

I believe that if you play sexiness deliberately, the audience
senses the phoniness and doesn't like it. It's something
that's in you or isn't. It doesn't really have much to do
with breasts or thighs or the pout of your lips.

SOPHIA LOREN

I suppose I'm fortunate that all of me looks like it was
assembled in the same factory.

MICHELLE PFEIFFER

I have eyes like a bullfrog, a neck like an ostrich and long, limp hair. You just *have* to be good to survive with *that* kind of equipment.

BETTE DAVIS

If I hadn't been born with them, I would have had them made.

DOLLY PARTON

What the hell is the matter with a society that feels compelled to ridicule any woman past the age where she's deemed sexually attractive to men? No wonder middle-aged women are going bonkers. First they're zapped by total hormonal chaos that gives them hot flashes and black depressions . . . and then society tells them that if they're not invisible, they're ridiculous.

CYNTHIA HEIMEL

I have everything now I had twenty years ago — except now it's all lower.

GYPSY ROSE LEE

When there's a bit of me I don't like, I change it.

CHER

If truth is beauty, how come no one has their hair done in the library?

LILY TOMLIN

BEAUTY IS ONLY SIN DEEP

I always wear boot polish on my eyelashes, because I am a very emotional person and it doesn't run when I cry.

BARBARA CARTLAND

All right: I'm young, I'm beautiful . . . but you don't *have* to hate me.

SEAN YOUNG

When people say to me less is more, I say more is more. You'd never believe how danged expensive it is to look this cheap.

DOLLY PARTON

Our culture has moved back towards beauty, while feminine ideology has not. I enjoy wearing cosmetics today, and shirts too. What I am trying to get feminists to do is to change with the times and recover beauty and our full sexuality too.

CAMILLE PAGLIA

Let's face it: there are no plain women on television.

ANNA FORD

People who don't have it think beauty is a blessing. Actually, it's a kind of sentence, a confinement.

CANDICE BERGEN

It is really a very hard life. Men will not be nice to you if you are not good looking, and women will not be nice to you if you are.

AGATHA CHRISTIE

WOMEN ON WOMEN

Ideally, I would like to have Candice Bergen's face on my body.

RAQUEL WELCH

I look like a little kewpie doll from hell.

CARRIE FISHER

> Don't lose your nerve
> about a curve
> that oughter
> be shorter.

TINA SPENCER KNOTT

I can tell you that there are many occasions when I'd happily swap them for something smaller.

SAMANTHA FOX

Everyone thinks we should have moustaches and hairy arses, but in fact you could put us all on the cover of *Vogue*.

HELEN DIRK, of the Deers women's rugby union team

I went through high school squinting because I was so self-conscious about the size of my eyes.

SUSAN SARANDON

They tell me a woman can't play snooker properly because of her shape. I tell them it hasn't stopped Bill Werbeniuk.

ALISON FISHER

BEAUTY IS ONLY SIN DEEP

I was the homeliest kid you ever saw. I was covered with huge freckles, and my hair was straw white and stuck out straight like a scarecrow's thatch.

PHYLLIS DILLER

We didn't have a lot of mirrors when I was growing up. We had one that was cracked – so in my mind's eye I'm beautiful and tall and thin and glamorous.

BETTE MIDLER

I am on a diet as my skin doesn't fit me any more.

ERMA BOMBECK

My legs have become very ugly. But then, what use would beautiful legs be to a woman of eighty-five?

REBECCA WEST

I knew that with a mouth like mine I just had to be a star.

BARBRA STREISAND

I do not say that I was ever what is called plain, but I have the sort of face that bores me when I see it on other people.

MARGOT ASQUITH

Plastic surgeons are always making mountains out of molehills.

DOLLY PARTON

FOR A FEW DOLLARS MORE

MONEY DOESN'T talk any more – it just goes without saying.

Joyce Jillson once said: 'A woman can't be too rich, too thin, or have too many silk blouses.' The trouble is, even if you *are* rich, beautiful lucre has a rather disconcerting habit of, er, disappearing. Overnight, in fact. And without you having anything to show for it the next morning. Except, maybe, a hangover.

Rich people may never get to heaven, but paupers are already serving their time in hell on this earth. Or as Mae West put it: 'Virtue may be its own reward, but it doesn't bring in much at the box office.'

Sometimes newspapers run articles called 'Money Matters'. Does anyone imagine it doesn't? 'The two most beautiful words in the English language,' said Dorothy Parker, 'are "Cheque enclosed".' Filthy lucre, not the Grim Reaper, is the great leveller. It's where all the boundaries of class and social distinction disappear. Most of us have pipe dreams about getting out of dead-end jobs and retiring to Malibu to lie in the sun, but for most of us, that is what they remain – pipe dreams.

Economists, not politicians, run the world. The best things in life may be free, but you can enjoy them more if you're better off. Money may not be able to buy happiness, but it sure as hell (or heaven) can make a sizeable down payment on it. It may not buy friends either, but it will get you a better class of enemy. And if someone tells you it can't buy love, tell them this may be so, but love can't buy money either.

Mary Tyler Moore once made a profound comment on the fo£ding $tuff: 'Three things helped me to get through life successfully,' she said. 'An understanding husband, an extremely good analyst . . . and millions and millions of dollars.'

A lot of people have made money out of me, and I've decided I'm going to be one of them.

JOAN COLLINS

Women prefer men to have something tender about them – especially the legal kind.

KAY INGRAM

A fool and his money are soon married.

CAROLYN WELLS

If someone was stupid enough to offer me a million dollars to make a picture, I was certainly not dumb enough to turn it down.

ELIZABETH TAYLOR

What I know about money I learned the hard way — by having it.

MARGARET HALSEY

We women ought to put first things first. Why should we mind if men have their faces on the money as long as we get our hands on it?

IVY BAKER PRIEST

Anyone who's ever struggled with poverty knows how extremely expensive it is to be poor.

HYLDA BAKER

A credit card is an anaesthetic which simply delays the pain.

HELEN MASON

Having money is like being blonde. It's more fun but not vital.

MARY QUANT

After the rich, the most obnoxious people in the world are those that *serve* the rich.

EDNA O'BRIEN

FOR A FEW DOLLARS MORE

A little hush money can do a lot of talking.

MAE WEST

My consciousness is fine; it's my pay that needs raising.

PHYLLIS DILLER

The only thing I like about rich people is their money.

NANCY ASTOR

Millionaires are marrying their secretaries because they're so busy making money they haven't time to see other girls.

DORIS LILLY

People don't resent having nothing nearly as much as having too little.

IVY COMPTON-BURNETT

I know I can't take it with me, but will it last until I go?

MARTHA NEWMAYER

No one would ever have remembered the Good Samaritan if he'd only had good intentions; he had money as well.

MARGARET THATCHER

My mother's idea of economy was to take a bus ride to the Ritz.

LADY TRUMPINGTON

WOMEN ON WOMEN

If you don't have a lot of money, you think that people who do are luckier than you are. When you do have money, you think that something's wrong with you because you're not happier or luckier than you were before you had.

ROSEANNE

A gold rush is what happens when a line of chorus girls spots a man with a bank roll.

MAE WEST

What I call loaded I'm not. What other people call loaded I am.

ZSA ZSA GABOR

When I first started working, I used to dream of the day when I might be earning the salary I'm now starving on.

CAROL BURNETT

I was once so poor I didn't know where my next husband was coming from.

MAE WEST

When the bills come in, there are a number of things you can do besides cry. For one, you can fill in the form for Amount Enclosed . . . and then forget to enclose it.

PEG BRACKEN

Nothing so sharpens the disposition as anything which touches on the pocketbook.

ANITA BLACKMON

FOR A FEW DOLLARS MORE

Of course I despise money when I haven't got any. It's the only dignified thing to do.

AGATHA CHRISTIE

Anyone who makes a lot of money quickly must be pretty crooked; honesty pushing away at the grindstone never made anyone a bomb.

MANDY RICE-DAVIES

A poor person who is unhappy is in a better position than a rich person who is unhappy. Because the poor person has hope. He thinks money would help.

JEAN KERR

People who think money can do anything may very well be suspected of doing anything for money.

MARY PETTIBONE POOLE

Money is what you'd get on beautifully without if only other people weren't so crazy about it.

MARGARET HARRIMAN

Anyone who thinks there's safety in numbers hasn't looked in the Stock Market pages.

IRENE PETER

Hollywood money isn't money. It's congealed snow, and it melts in your hands.

DOROTHY PARKER

If all the rich people in the world divided up their money among themselves, there wouldn't be enough to go around.

CHRISTINA STEAD

The women who do the most work get the least money, and the women who have the least money do the most work.

CHARLOTTE GILMAN

Bo Peep did it for the insurance.

ANON.

I want a man who's kind and understanding – is that too much to ask of a millionaire?

ZSA ZSA GABOR

I'm successful because I'm a good businesswoman.

MADONNA

Sometimes when I was modelling I'd be walking round with as much as $25,000 in uncashed cheques in my bag because I didn't have time to get to the bank.

KIM BASINGER

Poor people are allowed the same dreams as everyone else.

KIMI GRAY

The only people who claim that money is not important

are those who have enough to be relieved of the ugly burden of thinking about it.

JOYCE CAROL OATES

What good is freedom if you've not got the money for it? It's all very fine to go on about Nora's escape at the end of *A Doll's House*, but just how was she planning to eat that night?

LILLIAN HELLMAN

A rich man is one who isn't afraid to ask the salesman to show him something cheaper.

ANON.

Just about the time you think you can make both ends meet, someone moves the ends.

PANSY PENNER

THE UNKINDEST
CUTS OF ALL

DID YOU ever feel like giving it to someone? I mean right between the eyes? Or, more to the point, between the *ears*. Sarcasm, according to some, is a kind of therapeutic weapon we can use to stave off stress. As Hollywood mogul Harry Cohn was wont to say, 'I don't get ulcers, I *give* them.'

The good news is that you don't have to join a gym or go jogging to let off steam. The bad news is that your verbal vitriol will probably make you an enemy of someone for life. If you're not one already, that is . . . Either way, the pen – or mouth – is still mightier than the sword. Sticks and stones may break your bones, but names will besmirch you for ever.

Not surprisingly, it's not *always* love at first sight between those who work (or even smooch) together on film sets. Greer Garson had such a horrible time shooting *Desire Me* with Deborah Kerr that when it was over and the critics touted Kerr as the new Garson, she invited that lady over, as she put it, 'for arsenic sandwiches'.

Bette Davis once said of a young starlet, 'There goes the good time that was had by all.' A contemporary echoed that with, 'Her friends say that she's in her salad days – others say she's not very concerned about the dressing.' And here's Dorothy Parker on a similar tack: 'That woman can speak eighteen languages – and she can't say no in any of them.' (Parker is also the lady who once wrote in a literary review: 'This book should not be tossed aside lightly . . . it should be flung with great force'.)

Rod Stewart is so mean it hurts him to go to the toilet.

BRITT EKLAND

Joan Collins' whole career is a testament to menopausal chic.

JOAN RIVERS

Princess Anne is such an active lass, and so outdoorsy. She loves nature – in spite of what it did to her.

BETTE MIDLER

Warren Beatty has an interesting psychology. He has always fallen in love with girls who have just won, or been nominated for, an Academy Award.

LESLIE CARON

I'd never make another film rather than work with Otto

Preminger. I don't think he could direct his little nephew to the bathroom.

DYAN CANNON

If Bo Derek got the part of Helen Keller she'd have problems with the dialogue.

JOAN RIVERS

Robert Redford has turned almost alarmingly blond. He's gone past aluminium; he must be plutonium. His hair is coordinated with his teeth.

PAULINE KAEL

The affair between Margot Asquith and Margot Asquith will live as one of the prettiest love stories in English literature.

DOROTHY PARKER

Why do I not like Marlon Brando? Because I don't enjoy actors who seek to commune with their armpits.

GREER GARSON

When someone sings his own praises, he always gets the tune too high.

MARY WALDRIP

Joyce's *Ulysses* is merely the scratching of pimples on the body of the bootboy at Claridges.

VIRGINIA WOOLF

THE UNKINDEST CUTS OF ALL

Don't worry about my husband: He'll always land on someone's feet.

DOROTHY PARKER

Some women pick men to marry; others pick them to pieces.

MAE WEST

Maureen O'Hara looks like butter wouldn't melt in her mouth – or anywhere else.

ELSA LANCHESTER

Tallulah Bankhead is always skating on thin ice . . . and everyone wants to be there when it breaks.

BEATRICE CAMPBELL

He was so crooked you could have used his spine for a safety pin.

DOROTHY PARKER

Nancy Reagan's skin is so tight, every time she crosses her legs her mouth snaps open.

JOAN RIVERS

Calvin Coolidge looks as if he's been weaned on a pickle.

ALICE ROOSEVELT

Mick Jagger never knew how to shake that bony little ass of his until he watched me strut on stage.

TINA TURNER

WOMEN ON WOMEN

My daughter's got a voice like chalk on a blackboard.
JUDY GARLAND, on Liza Minnelli

What a pity that when Christopher Columbus discovered America he didn't keep quiet about it.
MARGOT ASQUITH

Madonna's a woman who pulled herself up by her bra straps – and who's been known to let them down occasionally too.

BETTE MIDLER

Marilyn Monroe made it to the top because her dresses didn't.

ANON.

Madonna looks like a whore and thinks like a pimp. In other words . . . she's the very best sort of modern girl.
JULIE BURCHILL

Henry Kissinger's idea of sex was to slow down to thirty miles per hour when he dropped you off at the door.
BARBARA HOWAR

After my first night with Orson Welles, I looked at his head on the pillow and knew he was just waiting for the applause.
RITA HAYWORTH

THE UNKINDEST CUTS OF ALL

The English woman is so refined
She has no bosom and no behind.

STEVIE SMITH

I don't regard Madonna as a feminist. I don't think proving that you can be as stupid as a man is anything to be proud of.

SUZANNE VEGA

I'd have Edna O'Brien shot for crimes of collaboration in the sex war. The way she wears her romantic wounds — like Victorian Crosses. I bleed therefore I am.

JULIE BURCHILL

Liz Taylor is so fat she wears stretch kaftans.

JOAN RIVERS

One nice thing about egoists — they don't talk about other people.

LUCILLE HARPER

Millions long for eternity who wouldn't know what to do with themselves on a rainy Sunday afternoon.

SUSAN ERTZ

Don't put all your eggs in one bastard.

DOROTHY PARKER

Steve Davis is the poor boy who claims he prefers snooker to sex. Has he really ever tried going to bed with a cue?

DIANA DORS

WOMEN ON WOMEN

Parsons always seem to be especially horrified about things like sunbathing and naked bodies. They don't mind poverty and misery and cruelty to animals nearly as much.

SUSAN ERTZ

Place before your eyes two precepts, and only two. One is, preach the gospel and the other, put down enthusiasm. The Church of England in a nutshell.

MRS HUMPHREY WARD

Don't be humble. You're not that great.

GOLDA MEIR

One of the surest signs of the Philistine is his reverence for the superior tastes of those who put him down.

PAULINE KAEL

Even crushed against his brother in the tube, the average Englishman pretends desperately that he is alone.

GERMAINE GREER

Never worry about what you say to a man. They're so conceited that they never believe you mean it if it's unflattering.

AGATHA CHRISTIE

Never have I read such tosh as *Ulysses*. Of course genius may blaze out on page 652, but I have my doubts.

VIRGINIA WOOLF

THE UNKINDEST CUTS OF ALL

Most conversations are simply monologues delivered in the presence of a witness.

MARGARET MILLAR

His handshake ought not to be used except as a tourniquet.

MARGARET HALSEY

Marion Davies has two expressions – joy and indigestion.

DOROTHY PARKER

By and large I feel that most actors are like overgrown schoolboys playing at being men.

DIANA DORS

Marcia was incredibly organized. She folded her underwear like origami.

LINDA BARNES

When people play piano by ear, the left hand is usually quite unaware of what is going on at the upper end of the keyboard.

VIRGINIA GRAHAM

It is not widely known, except by those who worked with him, that Humphrey Bogart had a habit of picking his nose.

DIANA DORS

Feminist academics are politically correct stupid bitches.

CAMILLE PAGLIA

Marlon Brando is beautiful – but only from the waist up.
MARIA SCHNEIDER, on the set of *Last Tango in Paris*

The English think of an opinion as something which a decent person, if he has the misfortune to have one, does all he can to hide.

MARGARET HALSEY

To tell the honest truth, Clark Gable isn't such a good lay.

CAROLE LOMBARD

About as easy as it would be for me to nail a custard pie to the wall.
SHIRLEY MacLAINE, after she was asked how she would find it having Madonna for a sister-in-law

There is less in this than meets the eye.
TALLULAH BANKHEAD

Do driving examiners all have to imitate a Dalek when they speak? Please. Turn. Left. At. The next. Available. Turning.

MARY KENNY

At one time I thought he wanted to be an actor. He had certain qualifications, including no money and a total lack of responsibility.

HEDDA HOPPER, on a Hollywood hanger-on

THE UNKINDEST CUTS OF ALL

Diana Ross is a piece of liquorice in shoes. She walks into a pool hall and they chalk her head.

JOAN RIVERS

Poor Walter Winchell. He's afraid he'll wake up some day and discover he's not Walter Winchell.

DOROTHY PARKER

Sandy Dennis has made an acting style out of a postnasal drip.

PAULINE KAEL

I find people call it research nowadays if they ever have to look anything up in a book.

MARGARET LANE

Women give themselves to God when the Devil wants nothing more to do with them.

SOPHIE ARNOLD

I have nothing against undertakers personally. It's just that I wouldn't want one to bury my sister.

JESSICA MITFORD

He's the kind of man who picks his friends – to pieces.

MAE WEST

She doesn't know how to move, she cannot say her lines so that one sounds different from the one before. As an actress, her only flair is in her nostrils.

PAULINE KAEL, on Candice Bergen in *The Group*

WOMEN ON WOMEN

The trouble with Ian Fleming is that he gets off with women because he can't get on with them.

ROSAMUND LEHMANN

Bobby Fischer is a chess phenomenon, it is true, but he's also a social illiterate, a political simpleton, a cultural ignoramus, and an emotional baby.

MARY KENNY

Louella Parsons is a reporter trying to be a ham; Hedda Hopper is a ham trying to be a reporter.

HEDDA HOPPER

Charlton Heston has a bad memory: he still thinks he's Moses parting the Red Sea.

BARBARA STANWYCK

A good many women are good tempered simply because it saves the wrinkles coming too soon.

BETTINA VON HUTTEN

I wouldn't sit on Joan Crawford's toilet.

BETTE DAVIS

She looks like she combs her hair with an egg-beater.

HEDDA HOPPER, on Joan Collins

The Eurythmics are hippies with haircuts who stepped into the breach after punk. *Please* let them die painlessly in a plane crash.

JULIE BURCHILL

THE UNKINDEST CUTS OF ALL

You look rather rash, my dear; your colours don't quite match your face.

DAISY ASHFORD

He wore baldness like an expensive hat, as if it were out of the question for him to have hair like other men.

GLORIA SWANSON, on Cecil B. de Mille

It's funny that the two things most men are proudest of are the things that any man can do – be drunk and be the father of their son.

GERTRUDE STEIN

Freud's sole contribution to the twentieth century was to get rich doing what mothers, mistresses, whores and bartenders have been doing for centuries, free, gratis and for nothing: listening to other people's problems and giving bad advice to them.

SERENA GRAY

Sir Stafford has a brilliant mind – until it's made up.

MARGOT ASQUITH

He makes you feel more danced *against* than with.

SALLY POPLIN

Acting with Laurence Harvey is like acting by yourself – only worse.

JANE FONDA

WOMEN ON WOMEN

I never liked sailing men. They yell blue murder at you all day, but then when the boat is moored, the whisky comes out, Captain Bligh turns Casanova and is all ready to play deck coitus.

JILLY COOPER

The only consolation I can find in your immediate presence is your ultimate absence.

SHELAGH DELANEY

To understand Sam Goldwyn you must realize he regards himself as a nation.

LILLIAN HELLMAN

Prince Charles' ears are so big he could hang-glide over the Falklands.

JOAN RIVERS

Her eyes are so far apart that you want to take a taxi from one to the other.

BEATRICE CAMPBELL

Her age and most of her measurements were forty-four — not, you would have thought, much of a date for anyone but a cannibal planning a long voyage in a canoe.

KATHERINE WHITEHORN

That son of a bitch is acting even when he takes his pyjamas off.

CAROLE LOMBARD, on her husband William Powell

THE UNKINDEST CUTS OF ALL

It's not that we didn't get along; it's just that my mother-in-law is very objective. She objected to everything I did.

BEVERLY D'ANGELO

Devotees of grammatical studies have not been distinguished for any remarkable felicities of expression.

LOUISA MAY ALCOTT

Philip Toynbee has an unfortunate habit of collapsing under drink as though a sniper had picked him off.

JESSICA MITFORD

Malcolm Muggeridge thinks he was knocked off his horse by God, like St Paul on the road to Damascus. His critics think he simply fell off from old age.

KATHERINE WHITEHORN

CLEAN UP YOUR ACT

THE NECESSARY qualifications for being a good actress, said Dame Madge Kendall, are 'the face of Venus, the figure of Juno, the brains of Minerva, the memory of Macaulay, the chastity of Diana, the grace of Terpiscore . . . but, above and beyond all, the hide of a rhinoceros.'

Most people in the profession tend to demean and/or trivialize it – maybe as a defence mechanism. 'Who do I have to go to bed with to get out of this business?' pleaded Tallulah Bankhead. Peter Ustinov once likened it to 'being asked by the captain to entertain the passengers while the ship goes down'.

Katharine Hepburn believed it was life that was important, not art. Acting was 'just waiting for a custard pie, that's all'. On another occasion she called it 'the most minor of gifts – after all, Shirley Temple could do it at four'.

Cher made a similar comment a generation later when she said, 'You don't need to be smart to do it; just look at our last President.' Elaine Dundy said people were always asking her how she could say the same things over and over again, night after night. 'Don't we all anyway?' she said. 'So you might as well get paid for it.'

'You could put all the talent I had into your left eye and still not suffer from impaired vision,' said Veronica Lake, with disarming candour, begging the question: is that why she adopted the peekaboo hairstyle? Ava Gardner always insisted that actresses of her vintage in Hollywood were never required to act, just to *look* good. When the looks disappeared, you got 'character' parts – for which read B-movie roles.

I'm not very good at being me. That's why I adore acting so much.

DEBORAH KERR

I started out as a lousy actress, and I've remained one.

BRIGITTE BARDOT

It's better to appear in a good commercial in Japan than a bad movie in America.

VALERIE KAPRISKEY

If you're not careful, you may find you're making one film, and the leading man is making another.

ANN MARGRET

WOMEN ON WOMEN

I've played bad women and wicked women and they don't pay. If you play them too well, people hate you.

SIMONE SIGNORET

If I hadn't been an actress, I'd have ended up in an asylum, I'm sure of it.

MIA FARROW

A painter paints, a musician plays, a writer writes . . . but a movie actor *waits*.

MARY ASTOR

My mother was against me being an actress — until I introduced her to Frank Sinatra.

ANGIE DICKINSON

Acting was good training for the political life. The only problem is, the speeches are harder to learn now.

NANCY REAGAN

Scratch an actor and you'll find an actress.

DOROTHY PARKER

I do my best acting on the couch.

MAE WEST

You don't have to kill a king to play Lady Macbeth.

MICHELLE PFEIFFER

CLEAN UP YOUR ACT

Five stages in the life of an actor: 1) Who's Mary Astor?
2) Get me Mary Astor. 3) Get me a Mary Astor type. 4)
Get me a young Mary Astor. 5) Who's Mary Astor?

MARY ASTOR

Joan Crawford is the only actress to read the whole script.
The rest just read their own lines to find out what clothes
they're going to wear.

ANITA LOOS

Show me an actress who isn't a personality and I'll show
you a woman who isn't a star.

KATHARINE HEPBURN

I've a perfectly logical excuse for being a ham. Can you
imagine what dinner table conversation is like in an acting
family? You have to play the second act of *Hamlet* to make
anybody know you're there. You don't ask anyone to pass
the salt: you declaim.

IDA LUPINO

An actress is someone with no ability who sits around
waiting to go on alimony.

JACKIE STALLONE

Blond hair and breasts, that's how I got started. I couldn't
act. I knew how third-rate I was. I could actually *feel* my
lack of talent.

MARILYN MONROE

The only time I felt accepted or wanted was when I was on stage performing. I guess the stage was my only friend, the only place where I could feel comfortable. It was the one place I felt equal and safe.

JUDY GARLAND

My biggest fear is the 100 per cent performance . . . because after that the only way is down.

GLENDA JACKSON

Many actresses tend to forget they're women – and most actors are so self-centred they don't have time to remind them.

JANE FONDA

Doing a movie is like being pregnant: you've got that terrible long wait to see if it's ugly.

CAROL BURNETT

I always wanted to be a movie star. I thought it meant being famous and having breakfast in bed. I didn't know you had to be up at 4 a.m.

JUNE ALLYSON

I had no real ambition about acting, but I knew there had to be something better than the bloody chemist's shop.

GLENDA JACKSON

Acting is fun for me because I get to be everybody. I've been a pizza waitress, I've been a prostitute, I've died and come back to life – and who can say that, at the age of twenty-five?

JULIA ROBERTS

Until you're known as a monster in my profession, you're not a star.

BETTE DAVIS

Acting has never done anything for me except encourage my vanity and provoke my arrogance.

CANDICE BERGEN

I do a job. I get paid. I go home.

MAUREEN STAPLETON

Acting is a way of living out one's insanity.

ISABELLE HUPPERT

I don't understand acting except when I'm doing it. And sometimes not even then.

NASTASSIA KINSKI

One of the good things about working in television is that you know where the canteen is, and this gives you a great sense of security.

PENELOPE KEITH

Was she a great actress? Yes, I think so. Of course, women act all the time. It is easier to judge a man.

IRIS MURDOCH

WOMEN ON WOMEN

There are no small parts – only small actors.

GINGER ROGERS

An actor can remember his briefest notice well into sen-escence, long after he has forgotten his phone number and where he lives.

JEAN KERR

It's one of the tragic ironies of the theatre that only one man in it can count on steady work – the night watchman.

TALLULAH BANKHEAD

When I saw my first screen test I ran from the projection room screaming.

BETTE DAVIS

Actors between plays are like ghosts looking for bodies to inhabit.

GAIL GODWIN

Pray to God and say the lines.

BETTE DAVIS, on her philosophy of acting

I wouldn't want to do anything else – and, quite frankly, I'm not trained to. I have no other skill. I'm a half-assed typist, that's about it. It's like you come to a movie set sort of incomplete. You've left behind everything but a few books and a couple of pairs of pants, and you say, 'OK, I have nothing.' And they say, 'We have nothing either.' So you say, 'Well, let's stay together and then we *will* have something.' It's nice to complete each other for a while and be this big, extended Waltons family. And then when it's over, you cry and you hug . . . and they fade to black.

JULIA ROBERTS

TINSELTOWN
TURMOIL

HOLLYWOOD IS a place that was once defined as 'a trip through a sewer in a glass-bottomed boat'. Vicki Baum said the main thing she liked about it was that you could get along there quite well by knowing only two words: swell and lousy.

To make it in such a lunatic world, a make-believe personality is probably the most useful attribute. How else can one explain Katharine Hepburn's comment when she was asked about her marriage to Ogden Smith: 'What marriage? Was I really married? I can't really remember.'

Hollywood is a place where the only thing an actor saves for a rainy day is someone else's umbrella.

LYNN BARI

Hollywood believes it's better to have loved and divorced than never to have had any publicity at all.

AVA GARDNER

TINSELTOWN TURMOIL

If someone were to come from another planet and see the world through movies, they'd think it was populated by white men in their thirties who shot a lot.

BONNIE BEDELIA

To have a vagina and a point of view in this town is a lethal combination.

SHARON STONE

Hollywood is a place that attracts people with huge holes in their souls.

JULIA PHILLIPS

To survive in Hollywood you need the ambition of a Latin-American revolutionary, the ego of a grand opera tenor . . . and the physical stamina of a cow pony.

BILLIE BURKE

Working in Hollywood gives you a certain expertise in the field of prostitution.

JANE FONDA, after appearing as a hooker in *Klute*

Being a celebrity is a no-win situation: if you get along with your co-star, you're having an affair; if you don't, you're having a feud.

BARBRA STREISAND

Movies are so rarely great art that if we can't appreciate the great *trash* we have very little reason to be interested.

PAULINE KAEL

Hollywood's wonderful. They pay you for making love.

JANE FONDA

Hollywood is the only place in the world where an amicable divorce means each one gets 50 per cent of the publicity.

LAUREN BACALL

The movie business eats its young.

CHER

In Hollywood, you could make jokes about almost anything, including God and the Pope. But you could *not* make jokes about Louis B. Mayer.

RUTH WARRICK

I married before Olivia, won an Oscar before her . . . and if I die first, she'll undoubtedly be livid because I beat her to it.

JOAN FONTAINE, on her sister Olivia de Havilland

We're getting closer together as we get older, but there would be a slight problem of temperament. In fact . . . it would be bigger than Hiroshima.

JOAN FONTAINE, on the same sister . . . and the same problem

I don't spend too much time in Hollywood. I'm afraid I might wind up as one of Hugh Hefner's bunnies.

LIV ULLMANN

TINSELTOWN TURMOIL

In Hollywood, the girl throwing the bouquet at a wedding is just as likely to be the next one to marry as the girl who catches it.

GERALDINE PAGE

There are no *real* men in Hollywood. They're either married, divorced . . . or want to do your hair.

DORIS DAY

To win an Oscar, you must either play Biblical characters, priests or victims of tragic disabilities such as blindness, deafness, muteness or different varieties thereof – or alcoholism, insanity, schizophrenia and other mental disorders.

MARLENE DIETRICH

The quintessential Hollywood gathering is incredibly glamorous, jewels, fur, limos – accompanied by the stench of loss.

JULIA PHILLIPS

I am retiring, because if I don't abandon films, they may abandon me.

BRIGITTE BARDOT

It's the coldest town in the world. The people there would rather not be friendly unless you can be some advantage to them. Even the young set look down their noses at you. They'd rather not have good times than have them with nonentities.

ANN SHERIDAN

Hedda Hopper once came to my table in Chasens when I was having dinner with my husband and said, 'What the hell are you doing here? I've got a headline in the papers that you've broken up with Don and are in San Francisco with Glenn Ford. How can you ruin my big exclusive?'

HOPE LANGE

MGM wanted me to play a mother in a TV series but then insisted on another actress on the grounds that I didn't look like the motherly type. Whereupon I discovered I was expecting my seventh child.

JEANNE CRAIN

WISHFUL SHRINKING

ARE YOU one of those people who can't pass a fridge without making a commando raid on it? Who goes on a two-week diet and only loses a fortnight? Who steps on an 'I Speak Your Weight' machine and a voice says, 'One at a time, please'?

We've heard all the tired old gags before. 'I'm on a seafood diet. Whenever I see food I eat it.' 'I'm a weightwatcher. I like to keep it all in front of me where I can see it.' And so on. Maybe they'd be funny if we didn't live in a society that prioritizes slimness to such an insane degree. Nancy Reagan once said 'a woman can never be too thin', which is only one step away from that horrific definition of a woman as 'a diet waiting to happen'. The redoubtable Mrs Reagan nevertheless exemplifies a phobia that's exploded daily by the media to make us shed our pounds – both avoirdupois and monetary. In fact overweight is one of the few taboo subjects we have left, as is evidenced by the number of euphemisms we have to describe life in the fat lane.

Truly, life's a bitch. And then you *don't* diet. Or return to slender. In fact the twentieth century can pride itself on creating a society where a woman might well prefer a deadly disease than a pair of bulging thighs.

There's also the question of double standards. Only men are allowed to be fat and happy. 'There's more of him to love,' we hear it said. But rotund women are dumpy and blowsy. They've 'let themselves go'. Brenda Fricker said recently that when Robert De Niro piled on the pounds to play Jake la Motta in *Raging Bull* he became hero-worshipped overnight by all the Method-oriented critics, but if she put it on she'd probably be told by her agent to shape up or ship out. Exaggeration? Maybe not.

From the day she weighs 140 lbs, the chief excitement in a woman's life consists in spotting women who are fatter than she is.

HELEN ROWLAND

If my jeans could talk, they'd plead for mercy.

PHYLLIS DILLER

The best reducing exercise is to shake your head violently from side to side when offered a second helping.

KAY FINCH

You know you need to diet when they start to charge extra on the airlines.

PAM BROWN

WISHFUL SHRINKING

Let's face it: if your average woman knew as much about sexual politics as she does about the number of calories in a slice of cheesecake, then society would be a matriarchy.

SERENA GRAY

A diet is an all-consuming obsession with the food you shouldn't have eaten yesterday but did, the food you have eaten today but shouldn't have, and the food you shouldn't eat tomorrow but probably will.

SANDRA BERGSON

I feel about aeroplanes the way I feel about diets. They're wonderful things for other people to go on.

JEAN KERR

I eat when I'm depressed and I eat when I'm happy. When I can't decide whether I'm depressed or happy, I make the decision while I'm eating.

OPRAH WINFREY

I'm not a glutton; I'm an explorer of food.

ERMA BOMBECK

If you eat the right food all the time, you'll die healthy.

ANON.

Eat, drink and be merry, for tomorrow you may diet.

SERENA GRAY

WOMEN ON WOMEN

If you lose weight to keep your ass, your face goes. But if the face is good, your ass isn't. I'll choose the face.

KATHLEEN TURNER

I left modelling because it's no fun trying to keep yourself at 115 lbs when you like ice cream.

KIM BASINGER

A woman's body is in competition with every other female body on the planet as regards avoirdupois . . . and 99 per cent of the time she's going to lose.

SERENA GRAY

If I could be a lesbian I could have chocolate cake for dinner every night and still get laid. Men who have sex glands in their eyes and centrefolds in their hearts are strange, deranged, picky and exacting about women's bodies. Other women are not. Other women would be empathetic about cellulite and bad-hair days. Plenty of lesbians are fat and loved!

CYNTHIA HEIMEL

At fat farms and beauty spas one pays astronomical sums to be over-exercised and underfed.

PEG BRACKEN

Why am I bothering to eat this chocolate? I might as well apply it directly to my thighs.

RHODA MORGENSTERN

WISHFUL SHRINKING

Do I lift weights? Sure. Every time I stand up.

DOLLY PARTON

Never eat anything at one sitting that you can't lift.

MISS PIGGY

Food is an important part of a balanced diet.

FRAN LEBOWITZ

Looking up at my horrible ugly bulk on a huge screen was the turning point in my life.

LYNN REDGRAVE

Don't eat too many almonds. They add weight to the breasts.

COLETTE

When anorexics look in the mirror they see someone fat. So I'm an anorexic.

JO BRAND

I am not overweight. I'm just nine inches too short.

SHELLEY WINTERS

When I took Liz Taylor to Sea World, Shamu the whale jumped out of the water and she asked if it came with vegetables.

JOAN RIVERS

WOMEN ON WOMEN

For years I went to bed with pills and got up with pills.
It was the only way I could keep my weight down.

JUDY GARLAND

Give me a dozen heartbreaks if that would help me lose
a couple of pounds.

COLETTE

POLITICS IS FOR THE BIRDS

'THERE ARE too many men in politics,' said Hermione Gingold, 'and not enough elsewhere.' Former Labour MP Maureen Murphy said that the reason there were so few female politicians was because 'it's too much trouble to put make-up on two faces'. Or how about this piece of invective from Clare Boothe Luce: 'In politics, women type the letters, lick the stamps, distribute the pamphlets and get the vote. Men get elected.'

The balance of power has shifted somewhat since Ms Boothe Luce's pronouncement in 1903 – the world had still to witness the phenomenon of Margaret Thatcher, for instance – but her point still stands, in the main. You don't have to take office to sound off, however, and that's exactly what the following women have done. But it might also be worth bearing in mind the words of P. J. O'Rourke: 'Once women made it public that they could do things better than men, they were, of course, forced to do precisely that. So now they have to be elected to political office and get jobs as officers of major corporations and so on, instead of ruling the world by batting their eyelids the way they used to.'

A politician is a guy who'll lay down your life for his country.

TEXAS GUINAN

There's one sure way of telling when politicians aren't telling the truth: their lips move.

FELICITY KENDALL

I don't know a lot about politics, but I can recognize a good party man when I see one.

MAE WEST

If anyone accuses me of being a communist, I'll hit them with my diamond bracelet.

PAULINE GODDARD

The thing about a politician is, you have to take the smooth with the smooth.

SUSAN HILL

Ninety-eight per cent of the adults in America are decent, hard-working and honest. It's the other 2 per cent that get all the publicity. But then – we elected them.

LILY TOMLIN

POLITICS IS FOR THE BIRDS

The best way to get things out of a government is to back them to the wall and then put your hands to their throats.

AGNES McPHAIL

Politics are usually the executive expression of human immaturity.

VERA BRITTAIN

You cannot shake hands with a clenched fist.

INDIRA GANDHI

The trouble with being a breadwinner nowadays is that the government is in for such a big slice.

MARY McCOY

Communists all seem to wear small caps, a look I consider better suited to tubes of toothpaste than people.

FRAN LEBOWITZ

A communist should be tidier, and not make work for the servants.

CARYL BRAHMS

It is probably true to say that the largest scope for change still lies in men's attitude to women, and in women's attitude to themselves.

VERA BRITTAIN

The traditional figures of revolution – Rousseau, Karl

Marx, Lenin and others — were no great emancipators of women: they left their wives slaving over a hot stove.

SALLY OPPENHEIM

U-turn if you want to. The lady's not for turning.

MARGARET THATCHER

A leader who doesn't hesitate before he sends his nation into battle is not fit to be a leader.

GOLDA MEIR

I always had a weakness for foreign affairs.

MAE WEST

I owe nothing to Women's Lib.

MARGARET THATCHER

You can't be a feminist and a capitalist.

RUTH WALLSGROVE

It is a pity, as my husband says, that more politicians are not bastards by birth instead of vocation.

VIRGINIA WOOLF

I may not have been a great Prime Minister, but I would have been a brilliant farmer.

GOLDA MEIR

If you want to push something in politics, you're accused of being aggressive, and that's not supposed to be a good

thing for a woman. If you get upset and show it, you're
accused of being emotional.

MARY HARNEY

Politics will always be run to suit the male agenda. No
matter how many strides are made in terms of equality,
at the end of the day women are still primarily responsible
for the children, for their education, getting the meals on
the table, making sure the school uniform is ready for
Monday morning.

AVRIL DOYLE

My husband said that if I became a politician, it would
be grounds for annulment!

LIZ O'DONNELL

We could get quite a lot of governing done if it wasn't
for politics.

HELEN SIMPSON

Being an MP is the sort of job all working-class parents
want for their children: clean, indoor and no heavy lifting.

DIANE ABBOTT

As President Nixon says, presidents can do almost anything – and President Nixon has done many things that
nobody would have thought of doing.

GOLDA MEIR

Any woman who understands the problems of running a house will be nearer to understanding the problems of running a country.

MARGARET THATCHER

Lately I've been asked by interviewers, 'Aren't you afraid you'll hurt your career by being politically active and speaking out on things like nuclear disarmament?' That makes me laugh. If there *is* a nuclear war, I tell them, what sort of career would I have anyway?

SUSAN SARANDON

It is well known that the most radical revolutionary will become a conservative on the day after the revolution.

HANNAH ARENDT

Some Californian people with a lot of money came to me and said they'd support me if I ran for politics. I said if I could play six weeks in Vegas and do two pictures a year, I'd do it.

SHIRLEY MacLAINE

Don't vote – the government always gets in.

GRAFFITO

One does wish that there were a few more women in Parliament. Then one could be less conspicuous oneself.

MARGARET THATCHER

POLITICS IS FOR THE BIRDS

A country that can put men on the moon can put women in the constitution.

MARGARET HECKLER

Inside, I am twelve years old. That's why I've never voted. I'm underage.

SOPHIA LOREN, on her sixtieth birthday

What's the point of having a vote if there's no one worth voting for?

SHIRLEY MacLAINE

THE MOURNING
AFTER THE KNOT
BEFORE

LANA TURNER said she originally planned on having one husband and seven children, but it turned out the other way around. And then there's Jane Powell, who was a bridesmaid at Liz Taylor's first wedding whilst Taylor was a bridesmaid at *her* first. Considering how both of these damsels fell so much in love with confetti (did they keep the bouquets and throw away the grooms?) it was just as well, said Powell, they 'didn't continue the practice or it would have become something of a full-time job'.

Joan Rivers' mother once gave her some valuable advice. It went like this: 'Trust your husband, adore your husband . . . and get as much as you can in your own name.' Mickey Rooney was equally romantic. He believed in getting married in the morning. 'That way, if it doesn't work out, you haven't wasted a whole day.' And Arnold Schwarzenneger said he heard about a wife who was planning to divorce her husband 'as soon as she can find a way to do it that doesn't make him happy'. Doesn't the milk of marital kindness just take your breath away?

THE MOURNING AFTER THE KNOT BEFORE

Maybe Shelley Winters more than anyone else epitomizes the manner in which we've become totally immune to polygamy. When she came back from her third honeymoon, she said: 'I just couldn't understand why my husband wanted to come into the house with me. I was just about to say, "Thanks for a nice time." '

Mistresses get a steady diet of whipped cream, but no meat and potatoes: wives get the reverse.

MERLE SHAIN

To me it's much more moral to be with a man you love without signing a piece of paper than to be legally in an atmosphere of boredom than eventually turns to hate.

URSULA ANDRESS

Marriage is all right – but it's carrying love a bit too far.

TEXAS GUINAN

Would I consider remarriage? Yes, if I could find a man who had $15 million who would sign over half of it to me . . . and guarantee he'd be dead within the year.

BETTE DAVIS

A bachelor never quite gets over the idea that he's a thing of beauty and a boy for ever.

HELEN ROWLAND

I've always been different. Now that people are living together, I want to get married.

BRIGITTE BARDOT

Dahling, this time I married a lawyer so he could handle the divorce.

ZSA ZSA GABOR

The only really happy people are married women and single men.

MARLENE DIETRICH

I married a Kraut. Every night I get dressed like Poland and he invades me.

BETTE MIDLER

Why did I marry three times? It was for a day out in the frock – I really can't stand wedding cake.

JULIE GOODYEAR

At some point in a marriage – even the strongest marriage – one person or the other is going to get restless and have at least a twinge of a thought about sleeping with someone else. For some people, this desire occurs about six times a minute. For others, it occurs around age forty. The thing to keep in mind is that nobody gets into bed with the same person every night for a period of years and listens to them passing wind without at least *imagining* a more alluring alternative.

WENDY DENNIS

THE MOURNING AFTER THE KNOT BEFORE

You never really know a man until you've divorced him.

ZSA ZSA GABOR

The surest way to be alone is to get married.

GLORIA STEINEM

Every bride has to learn it's not her wedding but her mother's.

LUCI JOHNSON NUGENT

Never trust a husband too far – or a bachelor too near.

HELEN ROWLAND

Demographic forecasts predict that by the year 2000 the number of households headed by a single adult will equal the number headed by married couples. For the first time in history, marriage is becoming an alternative lifestyle! In the face of such lousy odds, the question men and women who are contemplating a long-term commitment should be asking themselves is not: 'Is this the person I want to spend my life with?' but rather: 'Is this the person I want my kids to be spending alternate weekends with?'

WENDY DENNIS

Second marriages collapse at twice the rate of first ones.

MAGGIE DRUMMOND

The happily married woman who has never had an affair of one sort or another is almost a nonconformist.

SHIRLEY ESKAPA

The trouble about most lovers is that they have a habit of turning into husbands.

DIANA DORS

A successful marriage requires falling in love many times – always with the same person.

MIGNON McLAUGHLIN

One doesn't have to get anywhere in a marriage. It's not a public conveyance.

IRIS MURDOCH

After a few years of marriage, a man can look right at a woman without seeing her, and a woman can see right through a man without looking at him.

HELEN ROWLAND

It is always incomprehensible to a man that a woman would ever refuse an offer of marriage.

JANE AUSTEN

I've only been married three times and had three or four lovers. On today's market, that's practically a virgin.

SHELLEY WINTERS

I never married because I would have to give up my favourite hobby – men.

MAE WEST

THE MOURNING AFTER THE KNOT BEFORE

It is a statistical fact that people with weak hearts are more prone to cardiac problems during extramarital sex than when they are making love to their wives. There is more anxiety, often coupled with heavy eating and drinking as a prelude.

CAROL BOTWIN

One thing I would like to know is: whose fantasy was it that a woman finds a husband and then lives happily ever after?

DIANA DORS

I would not marry God.

MAXINE ELLIOT, in a cable she sent after her engagement was rumoured

Snoring could be a real threat to a marriage, particularly if it's a snore that blows lampshades off the base, pictures off the wall and makes farm animals restless as far as fifty miles away.

ERMA BOMBECK

A woman who cuckolds her husband is still largely viewed as guiltier than a husband who cheats on his wife. And when a wife tells, she grants her husband the traditional authority to punish, whereas when a husband tells, he seeks from his wife the traditional forgiveness.

WENDY DENNIS

WOMEN ON WOMEN

I should like to know what is the proper function of women, if it is not to make reasons for husbands to stay at home, and still stronger reasons for bachelors to go out.

GEORGE ELIOT

Next to being married, a girl likes to be crossed in love a little now and then.

JANE AUSTEN

I married beneath me. All women do.

NANCY ASTOR

It is ridiculous to think you can spend your entire life with just one person. Three is about the right number. Yes, I imagine three husbands would do it.

CLARE BOOTHE LUCE

I don't think there are any faithful men.

JACQUELINE KENNEDY ONASSIS

I heard about this couple who met out of town, fell madly in love, gave themselves a year to attend to the annoying details of shedding their respective spouses, reunited in another city when the year was over, got married and remain blissfully happy to this day. Boy, was that story an anomaly!

WENDY DENNIS

It's better to be unhappy alone than unhappy with someone else.

MARILYN MONROE

THE MOURNING AFTER THE KNOT BEFORE

My boyfriend and I broke up. He wanted to get married and I didn't want him to.

RITA RUDNER

I am a very committed wife. And I *should* be committed – for being married so many times.

ELIZABETH TAYLOR

Next to hot chicken soup, a tattoo of an anchor on your chest, and penicillin, I consider a honeymoon one of the most overrated events in the world.

ERMA BOMBECK

When two people marry they become, in the eyes of the law, one person . . . and that one person is the husband.

SHANA ALEXANDER

For the most part, men remain stubbornly blind to the possibility that their wives may be messing around, even when they're merrily cheating themselves.

WENDY DENNIS

Each husband gets the infidelity he deserves.

ZELDA POPKIN

A man would often be the lover of his wife if he were married to someone else.

ELINOR GLYN

Being divorced is like being hit by a Mack truck. If you live through it, you start looking very carefully to the right and left.

JEAN KERR

Some women have affairs, but unfortunately I marry my men. It's funny that a woman can have twenty-five affairs and nobody says anything, but if she has four husbands she's terrible. I guess I'm just a homebody.

HEDY LAMARR

I'm not exactly scared of marriage. It's just that, looking around, it never works.

JULIE CHRISTIE

People die after they're married. They die and become so bourgeois.

JANE FONDA

It's bloody impractical to love, honour and obey. If it weren't, you wouldn't have to sign a contract.

KATHARINE HEPBURN

I think husbands and wives should live in separate houses. If there's enough money the children should live in a third.

CLORIS LEACHMAN

One marriage in four ends in divorce – the other three fight it out to the bitter end.

LUCILLE BALL

THE MOURNING AFTER THE KNOT BEFORE

It's difficult to tell which gives some couples the most happiness: the minister who marries them or the judge who divorces them.

MARY WILSON LITTLE

To catch a husband is an art; to keep him is a job.

SIMONE DE BEAUVOIR

The reason that husbands and wives don't understand each other is because they belong to different sexes.

DOROTHY DIX

Being an old maid is a bit like death by drowning: a delightful sensation after you cease to struggle.

EDNA FERBER

I believe in large families. Every woman should have at least three husbands.

ZSA ZSA GABOR

Before marriage a man will lie awake all night thinking about something you said; after marriage he'll fall asleep before you've finished saying it.

HELEN ROWLAND

Have affairs if you must — but don't marry them.

FAY WELDON

Bigamy is having one husband too many; monogamy is the same thing.

ERICA JONG

WOMEN ON WOMEN

Every time Liz Taylor gets laid, she gets married. Nobody ever told her you can do it and remain single.

LILLIAN HELLMAN

Getting divorced because you don't love a man is about as silly as getting married just because you *do*.

ZSA ZSA GABOR

I'd rather be a beggar and single than a queen and married.

QUEEN ELIZABETH I

When a girl marries, she exchanges the attentions of many men for the inattention of one.

HELEN ROWLAND

London is spattered with couples living in sin whose lives are just as dreary as those of the respectably married.

KATHERINE WHITEHORN

Marrying a man is like buying something you've been admiring for a long time in a shop. You might still like it when you get home, but it doesn't always go with everything else in the house.

JEAN KERR

I've had a lot of very good friends. I've always liked them too much to marry them.

LILLIAN GISH

THE MOURNING AFTER THE KNOT BEFORE

My first marriage wasn't happy. I chose him because he knew which wines to order and how to leave his visiting card.

JEAN SEBERG

I have never married because there was no need. I have three pets at home that serve the same purpose as a husband: a dog that growls every morning, a parrot that swears all afternoon, and a cat that comes home late at night.

MARIE CORELLI

A husband is what's left of the lover after the nerve has been extracted.

HELEN ROWLAND

My marriage to Joe di Maggio was a sort of friendship with sexual privileges. I found out later that marriages are often no more than this. And that husbands are chiefly good as lovers when they're betraying their wives.

MARILYN MONROE

Cinderella married for money.

ANON.

Marriage is a great institution, but I'm not ready for an institution just yet.

MAE WEST

Love is the quest, marriage the conquest and divorce the inquest.

HELEN ROWLAND

It was an ideal divorce: she got the children and he got the maid.

JOAN RIVERS

It was not a happy day for me when I found out about a Yale University study saying that women not married by the age of forty have a greater chance of being kidnapped by a terrorist than walking down the aisle to say 'I do'.

OPRAH WINFREY

Every man should have a wife – preferably his own.

ZSA ZSA GABOR

A husband is just as hard to find after marriage as before it.

ANON.

Why does a woman work ten years to change a man's habits and then complain that he's not the man she married?

BARBRA STREISAND

Being married to Greg Allman was like going to Disneyland on acid. You know you had a good time, but can't remember what you did.

CHER

THE MOURNING AFTER THE KNOT BEFORE

Before marriage she talks and he listens. After marriage he talks and she listens. After a few years, nobody talks and the neighbours listen.

ANON.

I'll never forget the night I brought my Oscar home and Tony Franciosa took one look at it and I knew my marriage was over.

SHELLEY WINTERS

What a holler would ensue if people had to pay the minister as much to marry them as they have to pay a lawyer to get them a divorce.

CLAIRE TREVOR

Marriage is the only war where one sleeps with the enemy.

ANON.

The wages of sin is alimony.

CAROLYN WELLS

Marriage is lonelier than solitude.

ADRIENNE RICH

I do a lot of thinking about how I am going to merchandise my kids. Frankly, in clear conscience, I don't see how I can let them go into marriage without slapping a sticker on their foreheads that reads: This Person May Be Injurious to Your Mental Health.

ERMA BOMBECK

I haven't laughed so much since my husband died.

ANON.

THE SORROWS OF THE MOTHERS

MOTHERHOOD IS perhaps the greatest blessing and the greatest curse ever bestowed upon womankind. The physical pain of childbirth may be intense, but it's nothing compared to the mental anguish that follows.

Families tend to be decidedly smaller today than heretofore, but that doesn't mean they're less bothersome on that account. Indeed, making that precarious odyssey from Here to Maternity is as fraught with minefields as it ever was. Victoria Billings once said: 'The best thing that could happen to motherhood already has – fewer women are going into it.' Is this true? Perhaps it's marriage she's thinking of.

It takes a woman twenty years to make a man out of her son – and another woman twenty minutes to make a fool out of him.

HELEN ROWLAND

I would have made a terrible mother. For one thing, I hate to repeat myself.

JOAN MANLEY

The only time a woman wishes she were a year old is when she's expecting a baby.

MARY MARSH

The real menace in dealing with a five-year-old is that in no time at all you begin to sound like a five-year-old.

JEAN KERR

'If you're doing your job properly, your children must walk away from you.'

JOSEPHINE HART

I love all my children — but some of them I don't like.

LILLIAN CARTER

If you've never been hated by your children, you've never been a parent.

BETTE DAVIS

Never marry a man who hates his mother — because he'll end up hating you.

JILL BENNETT

There's a part of every man which resents the great bossy woman that once made him eat up his spinach and wash behind his ears.

KATHERINE WHITEHORN

THE SORROWS OF THE MOTHERS

Mother is the dead heart of the family, spending father's earnings on consumer goods to enhance the environment in which he eats, sleeps and watches television.

VIRGINIA WOOLF

Good parents, when they realize they're guilt-tripping their kids, will stop themselves in mid-whine.

CYNTHIA HEIMEL

Be kind to your kids – don't have any.

GRAFFITO

No one knows what their life expectancy is, but I have a horror of leaving this world and not having anyone in the entire family know how to replace a toilet-tissue spindle.

ERMA BOMBECK

A mother is not a person to lean on, but a person who makes leaning unnecessary.

DOROTHY FISHER

If men had to have babies they would only ever have one each.

PRINCESS DIANA

I got so much food spat back in my face when my kids were small, I put windshield wipers on my glasses.

ERMA BOMBECK

Most of us become parents long before we have stopped being children.

MIGNON McLAUGHLIN

There's a time when you have to explain to your children why they're born — and it's a marvellous thing if you know the reason by then.

HAZEL SCOTT

Why do grandparents and grandchildren get along so well? Because they have the same enemy — the mother.

CLAUDETTE COLBERT

As a breastfeeding mother, you're basically just meals on heels.

KATHY LETTE

Sometimes being a mother really stinks. I'm in charge because I'm the oldest and the biggest, but there's no book of instructions.

CHER

The truth is that it is not the sins of the fathers that descend unto the third generation, but the sorrows of the mothers.

ANNE FRANK

When I decided it wasn't fulfilling me to clean chrome taps with a toothbrush, I set out to write a column for housewives. It was the only subject in life I could discuss for more than five minutes. Fifteen years later I'm still writing for housewives, but they've changed. I'm writing for a different woman now. She is no longer standing behind a curtain looking out. She has taken a bus and gone to town.

ERMA BOMBECK

TIME'S WINGED CHARIOT

IN DAYS of yore they used to equate seniority with wisdom, but today the prospect of ageing is more likely to send people into a tailspin. Things have now reached such a pass that women are going to enormous lengths to try to preserve their youthful looks. They may not, like Dorian Gray, have a picture in the attic, but they do have the phone number of their local friendly plastic surgeon – and any number of cosmetic aids to diminish the coruscating effect of Father Time.

'Old age isn't so bad,' said Doris Day, 'when you consider the alternative!' But she also said: 'The worst thing about middle age is the knowledge that you're going to grow out of it.'

Robert Frost once defined a diplomat as a man who remembered a woman's birthday but not her age. Oscar Wilde said, 'No man should ever trust a woman who tells him her real age; a woman who tells you that – will tell you anything.' Such sentiments, unfortunately, endorse the common clichés about ageing. I prefer Brigitte Bardot's

'It's sad to grow old, but nice to ripen.' Or Anna Magnani's 'Don't retouch my wrinkles – it took me so long to earn them.'

When you're old, everything you do is sort of a miracle.

MILLICENT FENWICK

People ought to be either one of two things: young or old. No, what's the use of fooling? People ought to be either one of two things: young or dead.

DOROTHY PARKER

I hate to tell you how old I am, but I reached the age of consent 75,000 consents ago.

SHELLEY WINTERS

No it's not great being over fifty. It's like going to the guillotine.

ANGIE DICKINSON

I'm not like Jane Fonda or any of those other women who say how fabulous they think it is to turn forty. I think it's a crock of shit.

CHER

At forty, a woman is just about old enough to start looking younger.

KATHERINE WHITEHORN

Allow me to put the record straight. I'm forty-six, and have been for some years past.

ERICA JONG

As a graduate of the Zsa Zsa Gabor School of Creative Mathematics, I honestly do not know how old I am.

ERMA BOMBECK

A man is as old as the woman he's feeling.

SOPHIA LOREN

The years a woman subtracts from her age aren't lost — they're added on to other women's.

DIANE DE POITIERS

Thirty is a nice age for a woman — especially if she happens to be forty.

PHYLLIS DILLER

I refuse to admit I'm more than fifty-two, even if that makes my sons illegitimate.

NANCY ASTOR

If you survive long enough you're revered — rather like an old building.

KATHARINE HEPBURN

Nowadays, when a fan runs up to me it's not to get my autograph, but to have closer look at the wrinkles.

ELIZABETH TAYLOR

The lovely thing about being forty is that you appreciate 25-year-old men more.

COLLEEN McCULLOUGH

I'm forty-eight. When I get up in the morning, I find my face hanging on to the end of the bed.

JILL GASCOIGNE

As long as you can still be disappointed, you're still young.

JOYCE CARY

When a man of forty falls in love with a girl of twenty, it isn't her youth he's seeking but his own.

LENORE COFFEE

I used to dread getting older because I felt that I wouldn't be able to do all the things I wanted to do, but now that I *am* older I find I don't want to do them anyway.

NANCY ASTOR

Women never have young minds. They are born 3,000 years old.

SHELAGH DELANEY

What is an adult? A child blown up by age.

SIMONE DE BEAUVOIR

The only obvious advantage to being an adult is that you can eat your dessert without having had your vegetables.

LISA ALTHER

WOMEN ON WOMEN

One of the hardest decisions in life is wondering when to start middle age.

ANON.

In youth we learn, in age we understand.

MARIE VAN EBNER ESCHENBACH

If you want a thing well done, get a couple of old broads to do it.

BETTE DAVIS

One wastes so much time – one is so prodigal of life – at twenty. Our days of winter count for double. That is the compensation of the old.

GEORGE SAND

It's just as well to be told you're too old at forty. Then you're over it.

GRACE MURRAY HOPPER

I believe in loyalty. When a woman reaches an age she likes, she should stick with it.

EVA GABOR

When I was young I was frightened I might bore other people. Now that I'm old I'm frightened they will bore me.

RUTH ADAM

The dead might as well try to speak to the living as the old to the young.

WILLA CATHER

People ought to retire at forty, when they feel overused, and go back to work at sixty-five, when they feel useless.

CAROL ANNE O'MARIE

Being over seventy is like being engaged in a war. All our friends are going or gone, and we survive amongst the dead and the dying as on a battlefield.

MURIEL SPARK

The secret of staying young is: live honestly, eat slowly — and lie about your age.

LUCILLE BALL

It may be true that life begins at forty, but everything else starts to wear out, fall out or spread out.

BERYL PFIZER

The only people who really adore being young are the middle-aged.

PAM BROWN

I'm at the age where my back goes out more than I do.

PHYLLIS DILLER

WOMEN ON WOMEN

It is obscene to think that one day one will look like an old map of France.

BRIGITTE BARDOT

Being seventy is not a sin.

GOLDA MEIR

When women pass thirty, they first forget their age. When forty, they forget that they ever remembered it.

NINON DE LENCLOS

There are no old people nowadays. They are either 'wonderful for their age' or dead.

MARY PETTIBONE POOLE

I would say I was ninety-nine, dahling.

ZSA ZSA GABOR, when asked what she would do if she lived to be 100

THE SCRAWL OF THE WILD

THE EMANATIONS of the prophet, as Paul Simon suggests
in his song 'The Sound of Silence', are perhaps as likely
to be found on subway walls as they are in burning bushes
or on marble slates. And, indeed, of the prophetess. For
it is here that the poet laureates of the disenfranchised
hold sway, the unacknowledged masters and mistresses of
agitprop outrage and semantic serendipity.

Don't worry about the menopause – worry about the ones
who don't.

I thought innuendo was an Italian suppository until I
discovered Smirnoff.

You can use a pill to get rid of a headache . . . and vice
versa.

Married men make the best husbands.

A woman who's smart enough to ask a man's advice isn't dumb enough to take it.

Adam met Eve and turned over a new leaf.

Oedipus was the first man to bridge the generation gap.

Little Red Riding Hood is a Russian contraceptive.

All feminists should be put behind bras.

Sex is the only game which becomes less interesting when played for money.

Marriage is the process of discovering the kind of woman your husband would have preferred.

Better to have loved a small man than never to have loved a tall.

Sex Appeal: give generously.

Veni, Vidi. VD.

Ah, well, at least life is only temporary.

We didn't invent sin: we're merely trying to perfect it.

THE SCRAWL OF THE WILD

Use contraceptives on every conceivable occasion.

Sailors always have a port in every wife.

God make me chaste, but not yet.

Pornography offers a vice to the lovelorn.

I like sex of one kind, and half a dozen of the other.

There are two times in a woman's life when she doesn't understand men: 1) before marriage, 2) after marriage.

It's not the stork in the morning that brings babies; it's the lark at night.

Husbands prove that women *can* take jokes.

Love means never having to say you're sorry; marriage means never having to say *anything*.

The most difficult years of marriage are those after the wedding.

The New Man will stand for anything – except a woman on a bus.

If it wasn't for pickpockets, I'd have no sex life at all.

Every man should have a wife, because sooner or later

something will go wrong that he can't blame on the government.

All husbands are alike, but have different faces so women can tell them apart.

A man who calls a woman a broad is narrow-minded.

Marriage is the only life sentence that can be commuted for *bad* behaviour.

The latest sex manual is all-embracing.

A yes man stoops to concur.

Women are the weaker sex . . . but men are the weakest.

My husband and I were blissfully married for twenty years . . . then we met.

Many a wife thinks her husband is the world's greatest lover; she just can't catch him at it.

The modern world has to be sin to be appreciated.

I'd rather have a bottle in front of me than a frontal lobotomy.

Coitus ergo sum.

A woman is never too old to yearn.

A LITTLE BITTY
THING CALLED LOVE

WHAT IS love? Is it a little piece of magic dropped down from heaven? Or – as some think – a disease, an affliction curable by marriage?

'Love is a fire,' said Joan Crawford once, 'but whether it's going to warm your heart or burn your house down, you can never tell.' As far as Mae West was concerned, love conquered all things 'except poverty and toothache'. And Joyce McKinney once said she loved a man so utterly: 'I would have skied down Mount Everest in the nude for him with a carnation up my nose.'

Speaking of flowers, actress Sophia Loren said that the two most important things in a relationship were 'red roses and . . . white lies'.

Love is much nicer to be in than an automobile accident, a tight girdle, a higher tax bracket, or a holding pattern over Philadelphia.

JUDITH VIORST

It may be love that makes the world go round, but it's the spinsters who oil the wheels.

DOROTHY ABB

I always say a girl should get married for love – and keep on marrying until she finds it.

ZSA ZSA GABOR

Real love is being able to let someone go. When you do that, they become closer to you.

EDNA O'BRIEN

Love is the drug that makes sexuality palatable in popular mythology.

GERMAINE GREER

It used to be 'Love Me Forever'. Now it's 'Help Me Make It Through the Night'.

ANNE TYLER

A woman despises a man for loving her unless she returns his love.

ELIZABETH STODDARD

If love is the answer, would you mind rephrasing the question?

LILY TOMLIN

Love is like quicksilver in the hand. Leave the fingers open and it stays. Clutch it and it darts away.

DOROTHY PARKER

A LITTLE BITTY THING CALLED LOVE

You need someone to love you while you're looking for someone to love.

SHELAGH DELANEY

Love, love, love – all the wretched cant of it, masking egotism, lust, masochism and fantasy under a mythology of sentimental postures, a welter of self-induced miseries and joys, blinding the essential personalities in the frozen gestures of courtship, the kissing and the dating and the desire, the compliments and quarrels which vivify its barrenness.

GERMAINE GREER

Love is blind, which is why it has such a keen sense of touch.

JAYNE MANSFIELD

Love is so much better when you're not married.

MARIA CALLAS

Nothing is better for the spirit than a love affair. It elevates thought and flattens stomachs.

BARBARA HOWAR

When a person is in love, he doesn't care about Biafra.

FRANÇOISE SAGAN

Love never dies of starvation, but often of indigestion.

NINON DE LENCLOS

Love is the history of a woman's life. It is an episode in a man's.

MADAME DE STAËL

Love is moral without legal marriage, but marriage is immoral without love.

ELLEN KEY

I live my whole life around my man – work, play, dreams, everything. When I am alone I am lost. I can only find myself with a lover. Some actors say they can only exist when they are playing a role. Me, I can only play a role, only exist, when I am loved.

BRIGITTE BARDOT

We had a lot in common. I loved him and he loved him.

SHELLEY WINTERS

When I adore someone, it's like an obsession unto the death.

BRITT EKLAND

Infatuation is when you think that he's as sexy as Robert Redford, as smart as Henry Kissinger, as noble as Ralph Nader, as funny as Woody Allen and as athletic as Jimmy Connors. Love is when you realize that he's as sexy as Woody Allen, as smart as Jimmy Connors, as funny as Ralph Nader, as athletic as Henry Kissinger, and nothing at all like Robert Redford – but you'll take him anyway.

JUDITH VIORST

A LITTLE BITTY THING CALLED LOVE

We don't believe in rheumatism and true love until after the first attack.

MARIE VON EBNER ESCHENBACH

I love you no matter what you do — but do you have to do so much of it?

JEAN ILLSLEY CLARKE

No one has ever loved anyone the way everyone wants to be loved.

MIGNON McLAUGHLIN

I'm going to keep on falling in love until I get it right.

ZSA ZSA GABOR

I don't want to live. I want to love first, and live incidentally.

ZELDA FITZGERALD

REEL SEX

THE SIGHT of two beautiful people writhing on a thirty-foot screen may bring pleasure to the audience, but often isn't quite as exciting for the performers themselves. Unlike in real life, they need to take into account the lighting, the position of their bodies in relation to the camera, the length of the take, their make-up, the fact that they might secretly – or even openly – abhor their screen lover, plus a million and one other circumstantial oddities.

'When I'm trying to play serious love scenes with her,' said Stephen Boyd of Brigitte Bardot on the set of one of her movies, 'she is busy positioning her bottom for the best-angle shots.' Michael Douglas went one better – or rather one worse – when he said this of filming *Basic Instinct* with Sharon Stone: 'When she scratches your back, you have to arch two beats and then roll over. Quite honestly, after the first ten or fifteen minutes of awkwardness, it's just marathon running.'

❧

REEL SEX

I'm in bed with Burt Reynolds most of the time in the play. Oh I know it's dirty work, but somebody has to do it.

CAROL BURNETT

I may not be a great actress, but I've become the greatest at screen orgasms – ten seconds heavy breathing, roll your head from side to side, simulate a slight asthma attack and die a little.

CANDICE BERGEN

The word 'Cut!' is a very cold shower.

KATHLEEN TURNER

He was extremely nervous. We cracked jokes, and it turned out I was the only one who hadn't done it in the back of a car before.

SEAN YOUNG, on making love to Kevin Costner in *No Way Out*

Making love on screen is really the most sexless and boring thing in the world.

JOAN COLLINS

It's intensely difficult to do a love scene in front of all these people. I usually end up sobbing in the dressing room after every take.

KATHLEEN TURNER

It's kind of hard playing a whore when you're walking round with a sheet pasted to your breasts like Doris Day.

SUSAN SARANDON, on *Pretty Baby*

WOMEN ON WOMEN

We had clean sex on the screen in my day. My sarong was thought very daring. But it seems like long underwear now.

DOROTHY LAMOUR

Audiences will get just as tired of people wrestling on a bed as they did of Tom Mix kissing his horse.

MARY ASTOR

I refused a part in *The Killing of Sister George* because I just couldn't see myself sticking my tongue down Susannah York's whatever.

DEBORAH KERR

The love scenes I did years ago were sensitive and romantic, but in today's lovemaking, couples are trying to swallow each other's tonsils.

LILLIAN GISH

There's more sex appeal in Barbara Stanwyck's ankle bracelet in *Double Indemnity* than all those naked bodies rolling around on the screen today.

BETTE DAVIS

I'll never strip for the camera. There are *some* people who should see you naked – but my high school teacher isn't one of them.

JULIA ROBERTS

LIFE, LOVE AND THE WHOLE DAMN THING

THERE WAS a time when not only the glimpse of a woman's stocking was looked upon as something shocking, but also the glimpse of anything resembling a brain. So much so, noted Freya Stark, that 'the great and almost only comfort about being a woman is that one can always pretend to be more stupid than one is, and no one is surprised'. Thankfully, such days are gone, and most women feel free to say what they think . . .

Actions lie louder than words.

CAROLYN WELLS

Life is all or nothing. Either you're a grey shrew of a thing, a reject, or a human beacon that people stop to warm themselves by.

EDNA O'BRIEN

WOMEN ON WOMEN

Happy people are failures because they're on such good terms with themselves that they don't give a damn.

AGATHA CHRISTIE

Jealousy is no more then feeling alone among smiling enemies.

ELIZABETH BOWEN

In real life it is the hare who wins, not the tortoise. Every time. Look around you. And in any case, it is my contention that Aesop was writing for the tortoise market. Hares have no time to read. They're too busy winning the game.

ANITA BROOKNER

It is better to die on your feet than live on your knees.

DOLORES IBARRURI

When one has been threatened with a great injustice, one accepts a small one as a favour.

JANE WALSH

Sorrow is tranquillity remembered in emotion.

DOROTHY PARKER

Human affairs are not serious, but they have to be *taken* seriously.

IRIS MURDOCH

Life is something you do when you can't get to sleep.

FRAN LEBOWITZ

LIFE, LOVE AND THE WHOLE DAMN THING

One does not love a place less for having suffered in it.

JANE AUSTEN

No one really listens to anyone else, and if you try it for a while you'll see why.

MIGNON McLAUGHLIN

A middling talent makes for a more serene life.

IRIS MURDOCH

One should only see a psychiatrist out of boredom.

MURIEL SPARK

Life is such a very troublesome matter, when all is said and done, it's as well even to take its blessings quietly.

MARY ELIZABETH BRADDON

Those who do not complain are never pitied.

JANE AUSTEN

If you live long enough, you'll see that every victory turns into a defeat.

SIMONE DE BEAUVOIR

When nothing is sure, everything is possible.

MARGARET DRABBLE

By the time your life is finished, you'll have learned just enough to begin it well.

ELEANOR MARX

WOMEN ON WOMEN

An ugly life is still preferable to a beautiful funeral.

KATHARINE HEPBURN

Life isn't one damn thing after another: it's one damn thing over and over again.

EDNA ST VINCENT MILLAY

Experience is a good teacher – but she sends in terrific bills.

MINNA ANTRIM

Life is something that happens while you're making other plans.

MARGARET MILLAR

Expect the worst and you won't be disappointed.

HELEN MacINNES

Above all remember this: expect nothing and life will be velvet.

ELEANOR ROOSEVELT

When you're on the periphery, it's not the periphery – it's the centre.

MARY ROBINSON

Life is the ultimate drug.

SANDIE SHAW

LIFE, LOVE AND THE WHOLE DAMN THING

If you think you can, you can. If you think you can't —
you're right.

MARY KAY ASH

People who think about the past have no future.

HERMIONE GINGOLD

Remember — no one can make you feel inferior without
your consent.

ELEANOR ROOSEVELT

Life seems to be a choice between two wrong answers.

SHARYN McCRUMB

The only difference between a rut and a grave is their
dimensions.

ELLEN GLASGOW

When you get into a tight place and everything goes
against you till it seems you can't hold on a minute longer,
never give up then — for that is just the place and time
that the tide will turn.

HARRIET STOWE

Nothing is interesting if you're not interested.

ANNE LINDBERGH

Eternity is not something that begins after you are dead.
It is going on all the time. We are in it now.

CHARLOTTE GILMAN

WOMEN ON WOMEN

Experience isn't interesting till it begins to repeat itself. In fact, till it does that it's hardly experience.

ELIZABETH BOWEN

There is no end to what you can accomplish if you don't care who gets the credit.

FLORENCE LUSCOMB

If only we'd stop trying to be happy we could have a pretty good time.

EDITH WHARTON

HOMME
IMPROVEMENT

IN CASE you didn't realize, we're living in a post-feminist universe. Which means that the egalitarian goalposts have shifted and folk are intent on *viving la différence* again.

'Women like to change men,' said Marlene Dietrich, 'and then after they've changed them they decide they don't like them.' Now that women have – at least theoretically – made men more PC and sensitive (if not downright wimpish) the question that remains is: does she like him? Or would she like the Old Man – or even, God forbid, the Old *Woman*, back?

I hate feminists. They've emasculated all the men.

CAROLYN CASSADY

Women have created the New Man – but then they suffocated and killed him when they found him to be unbearably unsexy.

KATE EDWARDS

When a woman behaves like a man, why doesn't she behave like a *nice* man?

DAME EDITH EVANS

I was never drawn to feminism. Feminists seemed to me to be very heavy, serious women who would never want to have anything to do with a light and trivial woman like me.

MARIANNE FAITHFULL

A career is a wonderful thing, but you can't snuggle up to it on a cold night.

MARILYN MONROE

I stand for what I call streetsmart feminism. If you have ten tequilas, wear a Madonna frock, and go back to some guy's room at 3 a.m. and are surprised when he makes a pass at you, well pardon me but wake up to reality and start living in the real world. For a decade, feminists have drilled their disciples to say that rape is a crime of violence and not of sex. This sugar-coated Shirley Temple nonsense has exposed young women to disaster. Misled by feminism, they do not expect rape from nice boys from good homes who sit next to them in class . . . sex is a dangerous sport. You cannot legislate for what happens or should happen on a date. The date rape thing has become propaganda and hysteria. If you have an unpalatable sexual encounter, so what? Big deal! You played Russian roulette and you lost.

CAMILLE PAGLIA

HOMME IMPROVEMENT

Girls are so queer, you never know what they mean. They say no when they mean yes, and drive a man out of his wits for the fun of it.

LOUISA MAY ALCOTT

I am glad that I am not a man, as I should be obliged to marry a woman.

MADAME DE STAËL

Women should remember that there are two areas where you must never criticize a man: his driving and his prowess in bed.

DIANA DORS

In response to changing female expectations, the New Man has been asked to execute a complete renovation of his psyche. He has been directed to transform himself from dull but beautiful breadwinner in the Ozzie Nelson mould, to androgynous danger-boy in the Mick Jagger mould, to caring, sharing and relating soulmate in the Phil Donahue mould, to risk-taker with a vulnerable heart in the Bruce Willis mould, to sensitive but sexy man-boy in the Kevin Costner mould.

WENDY DENNIS

If women got a slap round the face more often, they'd be a bit more reasonable.

CHARLOTTE RAMPLING

The resistance of a woman to seduction is not always proof of her virtue, but more often of her experience.

NINON DE LENCLOS

A successful man is one who earns more than his wife can spend; a successful woman is one who marries a successful man.

LANA TURNER

A bitch loves being born. It's her first experience of making another woman scream and cry and she likes it.

PAMELA STEPHENSON

Don't hoover under your husband's feet – it's grounds for divorce.

JILLY COOPER

In my observation, what generally passes for feminine camaraderie is more akin to conspiracy.

JONI MITCHELL

I don't mind being in a man's world so long as I can be a woman in it.

MARILYN MONROE

I envy men's naturally raucous sexuality. Male lust is the motor force of civilization.

CAMILLE PAGLIA

HOMME IMPROVEMENT

Twenty years ago, feminists set out to redress the inequalities between the sexes. Unjust laws and worse traditions had been foisted on us by men for centuries and we were perfectly right to be angry. Frequently, we still are. But somewhere along the line some of us have turned into boring, self-righteous, prissy old hags. A man can't say boo to a woman nowadays without first reflecting whether 'boo' is politically correct. He has to weigh every word lest he be reported to the Sexism Police – as if suppressing the word could suppress the thought. Our zeal for Correctness has become obsessive, arrogant and ludicrous. The mood of the nineties is a kneejerk reaction to the decadent eighties. We're hung over and extremely cranky. We are tetchy, bureaucratic and boring. This mood will change, of course. Moods always do. In a few years it will be OK to crack a joke again. But in the interim . . . ZZZZZ.

LIZ RYAN

What the behavioural scientists have discovered is that, while men *appear* to be the sexual aggressors, they are in fact responding to subtle signals that women – the clever darlings – are sending out. Women draw men to them through flirtatious behaviour: glint of eye, seductive posture, tone of voice, pressure of touch – the same gestures referred to as 'display' in the animal kingdom.

WENDY DENNIS

I love *femmes fatales* . . . because every women is fatal to every man.

CAMILLE PAGLIA

WOMEN ON WOMEN

Scratch most feminists and underneath there's a woman who longs to be a sex object.

BETTY ROLLIN

To me, the expression Ms means misery.

PHYLLIS SCHLAFFY

I'd much rather be a woman than a man. Women can cry, they can wear cute clothes – and they're first to be rescued off sinking ships.

GILDA RADNER

A lot of post-feminist thinkers seem to have burned their brains as well as their bras.

KATHY LETTE

Most women would rather have someone whisper their name at optimum moments than rocket with contractions to the moon.

MERLE SHAIN

When a man confronts catastrophe, he looks in his purse – but a woman looks in her mirror.

MARGARET TURNBULL

There is more difference *within* the sexes than between them.

IVY COMPTON-BURNETT

HOMME IMPROVEMENT

Women's Liberation is just a lot of foolishness. It's the men who are discriminated against. They can't bear children. And no one's likely to do anything about that.

GOLDA MEIR

The modern woman is easy to caricature – being devoid of hidden layers, shades or nuances. She is upstanding, confident and very correct. She works hard, she's ecologically aware, environmentally responsible. She wears cotton, flat heels, and a driven aura. She exercises, votes, saves, diets, campaigns to save the planet. She eschews alcohol, tobacco, fats, anything that might threaten her worthy existence. Her cosmetics are animal-friendly and scent-free, but she rarely uses them lest anyone think her frivolous. She is sexually informed and technically competent in bed – to which she usually retires at 10 p.m. If I were married to her, I'd shoot myself.

LIZ RYAN

It's better to be looked over than overlooked.

MAE WEST

Young women have a duty to flirt, to engage in heartless and pointless stratagems, to laugh, pretend, tease, have moods, enslave and discard. The purpose of these manoeuvres is to occupy their time, the time that women of later generations are to give to their careers.

ANITA BROOKNER

WOMEN ON WOMEN

Men lose more conquests by their awkwardness than any virtue in the woman.

NINON DE LENCLOS

Nobody is such a fool as to moider [waste] away his time in the slipslop conversation of a pack of women.

HESTER LUCY STANHOPE

During the feminist revolution, the battle lines were simple. It was easy to tell the enemy: he was the one with the penis. This is no longer strictly true. Some men are OK now. We're allowed to like them again. We still have to keep them in line, of course, but we no longer have to shoot them on sight.

CYNTHIA HEIMEL

I shrug my shoulders in despair at women who moan at the lack of opportunities and then take two weeks off as a result of falling out with their boyfriends.

SOPHIE MIRMAN

Some of us are becoming the men we wanted to marry.

GLORIA STEINEM

It's a fact of life that while men get to do the asking, women call the shots. Outside of rape, we control when and where seduction will happen. We do it when we're good and ready, or not at all. It's up to men to make us good and ready, though, and quite often it doesn't take a lot. We modern women aren't as prim as our grannies used to be. We still have our virtue, but we hardly ever use it any more.

CATHY HOPKINS

There are two kinds of women: those who want power in the world and those who want power in bed.

JACQUELINE KENNEDY ONASSIS

The Women's Liberation Movement has degraded us. Women were never equal to men; we were always miles above them. Men put us up on a pedestal always. We shared in a little bit of the glory of the Blessed Virgin – but now we're at an all-time low.

MEENA CRIBBENS

LITTLE DARLINGS

'I WAS born,' said Judy Garland, 'at the age of twelve on the MGM lot.' 'It was no great tragedy being Judy Garland's daughter,' said Liza Minnelli some years later. 'I had tremendously interesting childhood years . . . except they had nothing to do with being a child.'

Carrie Fisher confessed that she was streetsmart as a child – but the street was Rodeo Drive. And let us try to sympathize with the plight of Shirley Temple, who said that she stopped believing in Santa Claus the day her mother brought her to a department store and that gentleman asked her for her autograph.

Yes, children are growing up too fast today, and, yes, childhood is an endangered species, but are we doing anything about it? Maybe parents are too busy trying to keep ticking over *themselves* to worry about such a phenomenon. 'Insanity is hereditary,' said a beleaguered mother once. 'You get it from your children.'

LITTLE DARLINGS

A youth with his first cigar makes himself sick; a youth with his first girl makes other people sick.

MARY WILSON LITTLE

The quickest way for a parent to get a child's attention is to sit down and look comfortable.

LANE OLINGHOUSE

A man finds out what is meant by a spitting image when he tries to feed cereal to his infant.

IMOGENE FEY

If youth didn't matter so much to itself, it would never have the heart to go on.

WILLA CATHER

Get revenge on your kids: live long enough to be a burden to them.

GRAFFITO

A food isn't necessarily healthy just because your child hates it.

KATHERINE WHITEHORN

Most women want babies. Whether they want children or not is another question.

EDA LESHAN

I never meet anyone nowadays who admits to having had a happy childhood.

JESSAMYN WEST

I read a psychologist's theory that said: never strike a child in anger. When *could* I strike him? When he's kissing me on my birthday? When he's recuperating from measles? Do I slap the Bible out of his hands on a Sunday?

ERMA BOMBECK

Children should be seen and not smelt.

JOYCE JILLSON

How do I cope with my children? I have a big house . . . and I hide a lot.

MARY URE

Children, not having yet learned how to be hypocritical, are quite frank about pointing out their own merits.

VIRGINIA GRAHAM

A child develops individuality long before he develops taste. I have seen my kid straggle into the kitchen in the morning with outfits that need only one accessory: an empty gin bottle.

ERMA BOMBECK

Have you ever had that sneaking feeling that shopkeepers don't like children?

SERENA ALLOTT

All those writers who wrote about their childhood. Gentle God, if I wrote about mine, you wouldn't sit in the same room with me.

DOROTHY PARKER

LITTLE DARLINGS

A psychiatrist said, 'Be careful in the way you discipline your children or you could permanently damage their id.' Damage it? I didn't even know where it *was*. For all I knew, it either made you sterile or caused dandruff. Once I suspected where it was, I made the kid wear four diapers just to be safe.

ERMA BOMBECK

Oh to be only half as wonderful as my child thought I was when he was small, and only half as stupid as my teenager now thinks I am.

REBECCA RICHARDS

It's far easier to explain to a three-year-old how babies are made than to explain the processes whereby bread or sugar appears on the table.

DERVLA MURPHY

Parents learn a lot from their children about coping with life.

MURIEL SPARK

I have never met a child who did not feel that he is maligned, harassed and overworked – and would do better if he had Mrs Jones for a mother, who loves untidiness and eats out a lot.

ERMA BOMBECK

The main purpose of children's parties is to remind you

that there are children in the world more awful than your own.

KATHERINE WHITEHORN

No matter what the critics say, it's hard to believe that a television programme which keeps four children quiet for an hour can be all bad.

BERYL PFIZER

I've seen kids ride bicycles, run, play ball, set up a camp, swing, fight a war, swim and race for eight hours – yet have to be driven to the garbage can.

ERMA BOMBECK

A small boy at my son's school was had up before the head for being a cocky little beast and urged to adopt humility. So he did, for a bit. Then he lapsed into his old self. 'So how about the humility, then?' demanded the head. 'I was humble for a fortnight,' he said, 'but nobody noticed.'

KATHERINE WHITEHORN

KISS AND TELL

ACCORDING TO Marilyn Monroe, it feels very good – but it doesn't last as long as a diamond tiara. Maybe it all depends where you do it. If we compare a kiss to an electric charge, here's the respective voltage per location, according to a recent survey: kissing on a sofa gets 55 volts. The cinema is 66. A shag-pile rug is a whopping 625 volts, whereas a hotel lobby, for some reason, brings us up to 800. Department stores can range from 75 to 1,000, strangely enough, and under a wool blanket, similarly, can go from 250 to 4,000. They don't say anything about under the mistletoe – even if you spend nine and a half weeks there.

The same survey also revealed that the Lost Art of kissing is about to be revived. Because lovers, at long last, are starting to see it as an end in itself rather than foreplay for, er, Something Else. The bad news is that women are turning off the French kiss, at least as regards men they don't know *très bien*. (In case you're interested, zoologist Desmond Morris claims that the whole practice originated when mothers weaned their babies by chewing their food and passing it to their infants' mouths . . . so that now, when lovers explore each other's mouth with their tongues, they're really experiencing the primeval pleasure of a baby-feed.)

Another seminal difference between the sexes, according to researchers, is that 37 per cent of men kiss with their eyes open, whereas a whopping 97 per cent of females keep theirs closed.

I'm fond of it; it's part of my job. God sent me down to earth to kiss a lot of people.

CARRIE FISHER

Singers have such marvellous breath control that they can kiss for at least ten minutes without stopping.

JILLY COOPER

Before marriage a girl has to kiss a man to hold him; after marriage she has to hold him to kiss him.

ANON.

A kiss can be a comma, a question mark or an exclamation point. That's basic grammar every woman ought to know.

JEANNE BOURGEOIS

Tyrone Power was the best-looking thing I've ever seen

in my life. Kissing him was like dying and going to heaven.

ALICE FAYE

Kissing may be the language of love, but money does the talking.

ANON.

Harrison Ford is so famous he doesn't kiss with his own tongue any more – he uses someone else's.

CARRIE FISHER

Movie-making is the kissiest business in the world. If people making a movie didn't keep kissing, they'd be at each other's throats.

AVA GARDNER

Platonic friendship is the interval between the introduction and the first kiss.

SOPHIE LOEB

Frankly, I gave up kissing people hello at the age of seven when my mother hired a piano teacher who chewed garlic.

ERMA BOMBECK

Ask any hooker. Girls on the game will do anything for money – sex in any position, any weird perversion, orgies, you name it. But no amount of money will get them to kiss you passionately if they don't feel anything for you. And why? Because it's too intimate.

CATHY HOPKINS

WOMEN ON WOMEN

His kissing left nothing to be desired – except the rest of him.

ANON.

I always thought platform soles were something Alan Ladd wore to make kissing easier.

ERMA BOMBECK

DEDICATED FOLLOWERS OF FASHION

FASHION, AS somebody said, is gentility running away from vulgarity and afraid of being overtaken. The French moralist Duc de La Rochefoucauld added to that. 'A fashionable woman,' he held, 'is always in love with herself.'

I wear the sort of clothes I wear to save me the trouble of deciding what sort of clothes to wear.

KATHARINE HEPBURN

You can say what you like about long dresses, but they cover a multitude of shins.

MAE WEST

A love of fashion makes the economy go round.

LIZ TILBERG

WOMEN ON WOMEN

I dress for women – and undress for men.

ANGIE DICKINSON

My boyfriend says my dress is so tight he can hardly breathe.

ANON.

Women who dress to please men should know that they don't have to dress to please men.

MAE WEST

Girls wear less on the street today than their grandmothers did in bed.

BARBARA CARTLAND

For fifty years, pyjamas were manufactured almost exclusively in broad coloured stripes, which reduced men's sexual attractiveness in the bedroom to that of multicoloured zebras.

MARY EDEN

I like clothes on other people, but they seem to suffer a sea change when they get on me. They deteriorate with a very strange rapidity until one feels really sorry for them.

JOYCE GRENFELL

I base my fashion on what doesn't itch.

GILDA RADNER

DEDICATED FOLLOWERS OF FASHION

The trouble with most English women is that they dress as if they had been a mouse in a previous incarnation, or hope to be one in the next.

DAME EDITH SITWELL

Brevity is the soul of lingerie.

DOROTHY PARKER

When I worked with Audrey Hepburn in *The Children's Hour* she taught me how to dress and I taught her how to cuss.

SHIRLEY MacLAINE

Being so tall, if I wear Laura Ashley stuff it makes me look like a kindergarten child in time warp.

SIGOURNEY WEAVER

The idea of ski-wear is to look like a cross between subway graffiti and Papua New Guinea.

MARIA STERLING

Princess Di wears more clothes in one day than Gandhi wore in his entire life.

JOAN RIVERS

By actual count, there are only six women in the country who look well in a jumpsuit. Five of them were terminal, and the other was sired by a Xerox machine.

ERMA BOMBECK

WOMEN ON WOMEN

I cannot, and will not, cut my conscience to fit this year's fashions.

LILLIAN HELLMAN

I've never been one to go for the *look* of clothes. I'm more a girl of comfort, but sometimes that bugs people. They think: you're in the movies, you're supposed to look fabulous all the time. Well, you know what? Women come up to me in department stores and say, 'That does *nothing* for your figure.' 'Why, thank you,' I reply, 'I'll bear that in mind the next time I put it on!'

JULIA ROBERTS

I was dressed by a man who had evidently read his instructions in Braille.

BETTE DAVIS, on an early costuming experience

Happiness is the sublime moment when you get out of your corsets at night.

JOYCE GRENFELL

OOPS!

WE'VE ALL suffered from foot-and-mouth disease at some point. In fact, some of us are in the habit of opening our mouths only to change feet. The difference, however, between Josephine Bloggs and Josephine *Public* making a boo-boo is that, when the latter does it, the nation gloats. Indeed, no matter how adept a commentator you are, it's your gaffes that will be remembered – and dredged up ever afterwards.

Carol Decker excelled herself at a function once with, 'I don't think we're going to get an award tonight. I would hedge my bets and say no.' Rosie Barnes went one better with, 'A week is a long time in politics, and three weeks is twice as long.' And here's the inimitable Barbara Cartland introducing one of her revelations: 'I'll tell you one fact. It may be rather boring, but it's interesting.'

Penny Junor came away with not a little egg on her face when she said, 'Elizabeth Taylor was a far bigger woman than Richard Burton.' As did Gloria Hunniford, who, when interviewing a writer, asked, without any trace

of a tongue in her cheek, 'Did you find yourself remi-
niscing a great deal in your autobiography?'

So if you've got a birthday coming up in the next twelve
months or so . . .

LYNDA BERRY

This marks the end of a long life, and an even longer
career.

PAULINE BUSHNELL

Their stage act was one of the highlights of their live
performances.

ANNE NIGHTINGALE

I'm absolutely thrilled and over the world about it.

TESSA SANDERSON

She hasn't run faster than herself before.

ZOLA BUDD

I don't know what impressive is, but Joe was impressive
tonight.

MARLENE BUGNER

Homelessness is homelessness no matter where you live.

GLENDA JACKSON

OOPS!

T.P. McKenna's wife has a voice like a linnet, whatever a linnet sounds like.

EDNA O'BRIEN

The telephone operator told me there was no listed number for Bodiam Castle. 'Is it new?' she asked.

SUE ARNOLD

When Chrissie's playing well, I always feel she's playing well.

VIRGINIA WADE, on Chris Evert

There's nothing the matter with being sick that getting well can't fix.

PEG BRACKEN

Now is the time for both players to relax, take their minds off the game, and just think tactics for the next set.

ANNE JONES

Women really shoot billiards as well as men. We just miss more often.

DOROTHY WISE

Steffi Graf has a tremendous presence when you're standing right next to her.

VIRGINIA WADE

Of course Jim Morrison is dead now, which is a high price to pay for immortality.

GLORIA ESTEFAN

Working mothers are the backbone of the third half of the economy.

GLENDA JACKSON

Having a baby is one of the hardest and most strenuous things known to man.

ANNA RAEBURN

Half the population is aged over forty, not under.

LAUREN BACALL

We have every window cleaner's dream: self-cleaning windows.

MAGGIE PHILBIN

Navratilova believes in putting her head down and banging it straight across the line.

ANNE JONES

As grim headlines forewarned of World War II, the following item appeared in a Hollywood column in April 1939: 'The deadly dullness of last week was lifted today when Darryl Zanuck announced he had bought all rights to Maurice Maeterlinck's *The Blue Bird* for Shirley Temple.'

LOUELLA PARSONS

Greg Strange needs no introduction. He's motoring correspondent for LBC.

CAROL THATCHER

OOPS!

It's not that my concentration is bad; I just forget what I'm concentrating on.

VIRGINIA WADE

When I've played a good first set, I panic and start worrying about how I won it.

JO DURIE

One time I walked out on suspension for nine months and Jack Warner said to me, 'Please don't go, Bette, we've got this new book for you called *Gone with the Wind*' . . . and I turned round, leaned across his desk and said, 'Yeah, and I'll just bet it's a pip.'

BETTE DAVIS, bemoaning the fact that she might have
played Scarlett O'Hara on screen

We shouldn't let the government off the hook just when we have it on the run.

HELENA GOODMAN

It's obvious these Russian swimmers are determined to do well on American soil.

ANITA LONSBOROUGH

I believe you're a fourth-generation chef. What did your father do?

LUCY FREUD

Of the designs of mine that succeed, 50 per cent of them don't.

ZANDRA RHODES

HOME SWEET HOME

HOME MAY be where the hearth is, but not – leastways for the contemporary liberated woman – the heart. After generations of being chained to domesticity, she has walked away from her doll's house of oppression with nary a backward glance.

'Everyone's always talking about people breaking *into* houses,' wrote American playwright Thornton Wilder, 'but there are more people who want to break *out* of them.' George Bernard Shaw said that home is 'the girl's prison and the woman's workhouse'. That was in 1905. Ninety years on, has anything changed? Or has careerism merely doubled the domestic drudgery after the nine-to-five routine has been completed?

There comes a dreadful moment in our lives when foreign friends whom we strongly urged to visit us actually do so.

VIRGINIA GRAHAM

HOME SWEET HOME

I wanted to go out and change the world, but I couldn't find a babysitter.

GRAFFITO

It's amazing how many quick repairs a woman can fix with an ordinary kitchen knife where a man can't lift a finger with his tool chest.

TINA SPENCER KNOTT

I hate housework. You make the beds, you do the dishes – and six months later you have to start all over again.

JOAN RIVERS

Home is the place where the husband runs the show, but the wife still writes the script.

CYBILL SHEPHERD

This is an equal opportunities kitchen.

GRAFFITO

It puzzles me how a child can see a dairy bar three miles away, but he cannot see a four by six rug that has scrunched up under his feet and has been dragged through two rooms.

ERMA BOMBECK

When the loo paper gets thicker and the writing paper thinner, it's always a bad sign at home.

NANCY MITFORD

WOMEN ON WOMEN

I refuse to believe that trading recipes is silly. Tuna fish casserole is at least as real as corporate stock.

BARBARA HARRISON

I have trouble with toast. Toast is very difficult. You have to watch it all the time or it burns up.

JULIA CHILD

Heaven knows, home is a hard hat area.

ERMA BOMBECK

I'm a wonderful housekeeper. Every time I get divorced I keep the house.

ZSA ZSA GABOR

I'm not wild about holidays. They always seem a ludicrously expensive way of proving there's no place like home.

JILLY COOPER

The last time my family laughed was when my oven caught fire and we had to eat out for a week.

ERMA BOMBECK

ANECDOTAGE

REPARTEE HAS been defined as the *bon mot* you thought of on the way home from the party. Such dilatory wit wasn't an affliction of the following catchers in the wry, however. Would that we could all be this gloriously catty.

A woman said to Dorothy Parker once, 'I can't *bear* fools.' Parker replied, 'Apparently your mother didn't have the same difficulty.'

A young actress once said to Rosalind Russell, 'I dread to think of life at forty-five.' Russell replied, 'Why, what happened?'

Marlene Dietrich once said to her photographer, after scanning some stills she was less than pleased with, 'Five years ago you used to be able to make me look beautiful.' 'I know, but I was much younger then,' he said.

When Dorothy Parker heard that a certain English actress – infamous for her dalliances with members of the legal profession – had broken her leg, she mused, 'It must have happened when she was sliding down a barrister.'

Earl Wilson thought he'd insult Tallulah Bankhead by asking her if she'd ever been mistaken for a man on the phone. 'No darling,' she replied tartly. 'Have you?'

A wife comes home to find her husband packing his bags and she asks him where he's going. 'To Fiji,' he says. 'I heard the girls over there give you £5 to make love to them.' 'Hold on a minute,' she says, 'I'm coming with you. I want to see how you can live on a tenner a month.'

When Mae West was asked if she could be trusted, she said, 'Of course, ask any of my husbands.'

Dorothy Parker was asked to put the word 'horticulture' in a sentence and said: 'You can lead a horticulture, but you can't make her think.'

A lady said to Zsa Zsa Gabor, 'I'm breaking my engagement to a very wealthy man. He's already given me a sable coat, diamonds, a stove and a Rolls-Royce. What should I do?' 'Give back the stove,' was Gabor's advice.

A director made the following comment to Sarah Bernhardt about a fledgeling actress Bernhardt wasn't happy with: 'You must admit she has some wonderful moments.' 'Yes,' she replied, 'but some terrible half hours.'

When Dorothy Parker was asked if she would like to duck for apples at a Hallowe'en party she said, 'Duck for apples? Change one letter and it's the story of my life.'

An actress was once criticized for living with a (substandard) actor. Her excuse? 'You can't expect me to bite the ham that feeds me.'

When an admirer said to Mae West, 'Goodness, what beautiful diamonds,' West replied, 'Goodness had nothing to do with it, dearie.' (When another said, 'I've heard so much about you,' she replied, 'Yeah, but you can't prove a thing.')

When Dorothy Parker was informed Clare Boothe Luce was kind to her inferiors, she said, 'Where does she *find* them?'

Jean Harlow once approached Margot Asquith at a Hollywood party. 'You're Margot Asquith, aren't you?' she said, pronouncing the 't', to which the latter replied, 'No, my dear, I am Margot Asquith. The "t" is silent, as in Harlow.'

When Brigitte Bardot was asked, 'What was the best day of your life?' she replied: 'It was a night.'

On hearing that President Calvin Coolidge had died, Dorothy Parker said, 'How could they tell?'

When Bette Davis was told that a rumour that she had died was circulating, she replied: 'With the newspaper strike on? I wouldn't even consider it.'

When a male heckler called out to American feminist Florynce Kennedy, 'Are you a lesbian?' during one of her speeches, she replied, 'Are you my alternative?'

Jean Harlow was once asked how she liked to wake up in the morning. 'I like to wake up feeling a new man,' was her reply.

When Dorothy Parker was asked if she had enjoyed a party, she replied, 'Enjoyed it? One more drink and I would have been under the host.'

ANYONE FOR TENETS?

Do YOU ever feel that you're terminally bored by clichés? That you would like to rewrite the English language with all its tired epigrams and jaded metaphors? The following truisms — inverted and strangled out of shape — may point you in that direction.

Better to have loved and lost . . . than to have spent all your life with the bastard.

She who hesitates . . . is won.

A little yearning is a dangerous thing.

Love means . . . never having to say you're randy.

The way to a man's heart . . . is through his ribs.

WOMEN ON WOMEN

Where there's a Pill there's a way.

A leotard can never change its spots.

Cleanliness is next to . . . impossible.

Uneasy is the head . . . that wears the curlers.

A thing of beauty . . . costs a small fortune.

What every girl should know is . . . better.

Love and marriage . . . go together like a horse and carnage.

Georgie Porgie pudding and pie, kissed the girls and made them cry. When the boys came out to play . . . he kissed them too, he's funny that way.

Don't batter children . . . they taste better fried.

Youth is stranger than fiction.

A friend in need . . . is a bloody nuisance.

In vino headachitas.

Two wrongs don't make a right . . . but they make a helluva good excuse.

ANYONE FOR TENETS?

People who smile when things go wrong . . . have found someone to blame it on.

Boys will be boys . . . because lately the girls are gaining on them.

Absence makes the heart . . . go wander.

Children brighten a home . . . because they keep leaving the bloody lights on.

An apple a day keeps the doctor away . . . and an onion a day keeps everyone away.

Charity begins at home . . . and generally gets no further.

The meek shall inherit the earth . . . because nobody else would tolerate the ridiculous inheritance taxes.

If the cap fits . . . it's probably out of fashion.

Eat, drink and be merry . . . tomorrow we may be radio-active.

Everything comes to he who waits . . . except a bus.

A bird in the hand . . . invariably does something unmentionable on your wrist.

Hell hath no fury . . . like vested interest masquerading as moral principle.

Power corrupts; absolute power . . . is even more fun.

Jesus saves . . . but then he's not on PAYE.

The hand that rocks the cradle . . . gets extremely tired.

If at first you don't succeed . . . give it up as a bad job.

He who laughs last . . . is a nerd who's just got the joke.

People who live in glass houses . . . often get approached by double-glazing salesmen.

Cleanliness is next to godliness . . . in those dictionaries that don't know anything about the alphabet.

His bark is worse than his bite . . . if he's been eating garlic.

Sticks and stones may break my bones . . . and not only that, you'll be hearing from my solicitor.

The lion and the calf shall lie down together . . . but the calf probably won't get very much sleep.

I wandered lonely as a cloud . . . because I had BO.

ANYONE FOR TENETS?

Out of the mouths of babes . . . come things you wouldn't really want the neighbours to hear.

God is the answer . . . yes, but what's the question?

I think, therefore I am . . . I think.

The meek shall inherit the earth . . . that's why we call them worms.

Humpty Dumpty sat on the wall, Humpty Dumpty had a great fall, All the king's horses and all the king's men . . . had scrambled egg for a fortnight.

When all is said and done . . . more is said than done.

The good dye young.

Two heads are better than one . . . unless he's an expensive hairdresser.

You're never too old to learn . . . which is why most of us keep putting it off.

Many wise words are spoken in jest . . . but many more stupid ones are said in earnest.

Nothing recedes like success.

He who gropes and runs away ... lives to grope another day.

Too many cooks spoil the ... figure.

Familiarity breeds.

Love your neighbour ... but don't get caught.

To err is human ... to really foul things up requires a computer.

Crime doesn't pay ... but then neither does working for a living.

This, above all, to thine own self be true, and it must follow, as the night the day ... you'll die a pauper.

All's well that ends ...

EXEUNT

THE PROSPECT of death, they say, has a habit of concentrating the mind wonderfully – a fact to which the following quotes attest.

I am fed up. I am desperate and unhappy. I am suffering and I may as well suffer for something. So long, B.B.

BRIGITTE BARDOT, in a suicide note

All my possessions for a moment of time.

QUEEN ELIZABETH I

Is everybody happy? I want everybody to be happy. I know I'm happy.

ETHEL BARRYMORE

Next week or next month or next year I'll kill myself.

WOMEN ON WOMEN

But I might as well last out my month's rent, which has been paid up, and my credit for breakfast in the morning.

JEAN RHYS

Farewell, my friends, I am going to glory.

ISADORA DUNCAN

INDEX

INDEX

INDEX

WOMEN ON WOMEN